C000098523

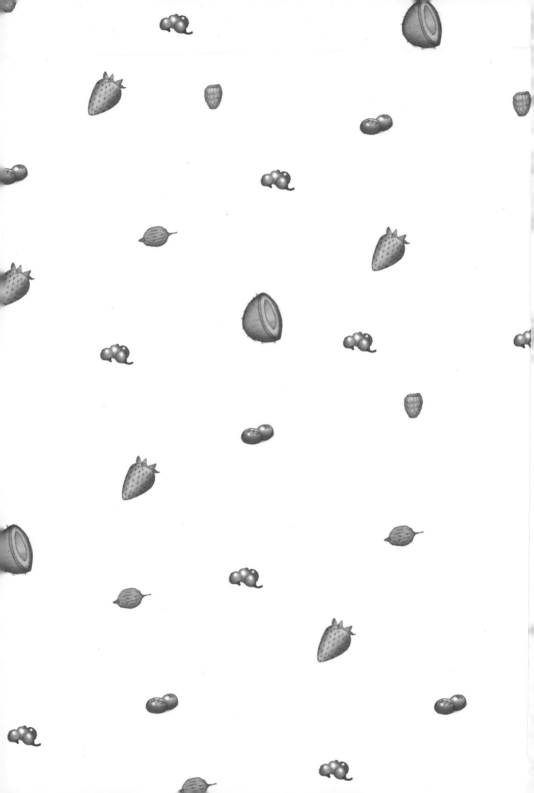

Everyone Deserves Dessert

By Matthew Caruana

Printed in England by CDP www.cdp.co.uk

ISBN: 978-1-5272-5329-2

Acknowledgements

Helena and Mark Illingworth for your brutal honesty about my recipes, for your discerning palettes, and for bringing me up "proper".

Peter Lee for help with many things and for allowing me somewhere to cook.

The Monday nighters for the many taste tests and comments: Fred Caruana, Jason Peachey, Ben Peachey, Graham Skelton and Beccy Higgs and for being awesome friends.

Sam Townsend for his expertise and advice on diets and generally being legendary.

Charlie Bristow of Black sky visuals for the superb pictures.

The Campbells of New Zealand who let me experiment and get paid for it.

Terry Herbert and Kevin Ratcliffe for their training and guidance all those years ago, for being great friends and for turning a strange boy into a Chef.

Gemma Middleton for her invaluable help and advice.

Louise for all her love, support and understanding.

The generous people at Churchill for providing some of their beautiful china.

Recipes

About me

Food has been centre stage in my life since before I can remember. I was born in Wales where we had a small farm with pigs, jersey cows and some chickens. My mother used to make cheeses and clotted cream with our cows' milk and when it snowed heavily my father would go out into the fields to dig out the neighbour's sheep with a baby me in one arm.

By the time I was learning to drive I had become one of the "fat kids" at our school and was teased mercilessly.

After studying Biochemistry at university, I had lost that weight and become quite fit. Whereupon I needed a job and found one washing dishes in a hotel. As with many Chefs I started in the "dish pit" and saw the men and women in white as something like rock stars, charging round the kitchen, shouting esoteric French words and wielding razor sharp blades like they were no danger at all.

I got the chance to work alongside these legends in an industry that I saw as honourable, doing real hard work and giving others pleasure. I declared that I wanted to learn the pastry section and was well shepherded in that direction.

Later I got my first Sous Chef job and moved further into the world of savoury foods. By this time the several Crème Brulée breakfasts I had enjoyed had taken their toll and some weight had crept back on.

During all this I had been diagnosed with some serious health issues and began the slow process to find out what medication would best treat my maladies.

I learned about ketogenic diets from a bodybuilder friend and would "cut" for a few months at a time and then go back to my unhealthy ways until I needed to shed that weight again.

By the time I had been a Head Chef in New Zealand and returned to the United Kingdom my weight was more than it had ever been and even with the ketogenic cycling it seemed I couldn't stop gaining weight overall.

I looked more heavily into diet, nutrition and exercise and started some furious gym going but at just short of twenty-five stone I was clearly missing something.

One night in bed I stumbled across some information about the effect of a very low carbohydrate diet on brain chemistry and realised that it was probably able to replicate the benefits of one of my medications without the constant hunger and lack of satiety.

I stopped taking one of the medications I had been prescribed for most of my adult life and started a very low carb diet in earnest. I decided to take a rest from the gym and with diet alone I lost 120 pounds in eight months.

It turned out that the medication had made me foggy, forgetful and confused and I had thought that it was normal. Now that fog was lifted and with the cognitive benefits of the low carb diet combined with the lack of this pharmaceutical it was as if I was a new man. The benefits were so many it would be difficult to list.

The rest of the story is straightforward really, I used my knowledge to create a few sugar free desserts for myself and eventually someone suggested that I write a book. I saw that I might be able to use my skills, experience and knowledge to really help people and not just help them satisfy their hunger.

These days, I am still a professional Chef and I still do eighty hour working weeks on occasion, but I also get to help people some of the time too.

About this book

This book started as quite a selfish endeavour: I simply wanted versions of my favourite desserts that I could eat without the sugar. It quickly turned from one lemon tart into a mission to bring decent classic dessert recipes to struggling diabetics and sugar free types.

I was frustrated by the lack of actual dessert recipes I saw that tended to lean towards fat bombs and different cakes and such. I found it annoying that there weren't any books on sweet low carbohydrate things that I would recognise from my tenure in restaurants and hotels. Most people had to use recipes from the United States, Canada, Australia and South Africa with loads of less common ingredients, and with everything in cups, not realising that there are at least three measuring cup systems that are all different. Therefore, I have presented everything I can in grams. On the subject of ingredients, I decided to use only items I could find in the three small supermarkets in my town and to stay as true to the original dishes as possible, using more modern components strictly when necessary. During the writing of this book I moved to an even smaller town with only one supermarket and I have attempted to simplify the ingredient list even further.

I've tried to keep the carbohydrates as low as possible, and this has led me to eliminate recipes that aren't practical as versions in what I consider a very low carb range of up to around 10%. This has therefore led me to specific ingredients which I will discuss later. I also chose to use one ubiquitous sweetener in all the recipes for purposes of standardisation. Later, I added a few recipes for things that are a little outside this range for people who simply want to avoid sugar or for people to eat on a "cheat day", so please check the carbs for each recipe before making it.

I haven't upped the fat content of the recipes just for the sake of it, in fact I have reduced the fat content in most instances. This is to make the recipes more available to everyone, so that if a family shares a dessert from this book none of its members might be eating harmful levels of sugars or fats or anything else.

I have intentionally kept the levels of sweetener as low as possible, so that people not used to the stuff can still gorge themselves on a bucket of chocolate mousse and not regret it the next day. This means that you may need to adjust the sweetness if you have a particular affinity for that taste, especially as I actually don't have much of a sweet tooth myself!

I had intended to give a list of the net carbs for the recipes in the back of the book as a guide, but after some brief research, the possible variation caused by using ingredients different to mine turned out to be so large that I decided this could be dangerously misleading. Please work out the values of each recipe according to the specific ingredients that you use.

Feel free to combine these recipes with elements from elsewhere like shop bought low carb pastry or a pastry recipe from another source. Even with all my efforts, several others are still superior to mine.

This book, as any recipe book, is intended as a starting point for you, not a definitive set of rules. Recipes are constantly evolving, and everyone's palette is different. Produce changes from plant to plant and field to field, even two lemons on the same tree will taste slightly different. Taste as much as you can and change the recipes to suit you. The ratios and weights are the important bit, but again experiment and make it work for you.

For diabetics

To help make the recipes more diabetic friendly I have included notes for some recipes on how to reduce the fat and already lowered it in others. Some of the recipes that are based on classical French and British recipes use a lot of fat which is intrinsic to the recipe and these therefore don't have notes on replacing ingredients. If a recipe is too high in fat for you, simply choose a different one or make your own version with other ingredients, these recipes are just well tested suggestions, you are in charge.

If you don't fancy the salt in some of the recipes, just don't put it in, but I would recommend leaving it in if it's a chocolate-based recipe. Trust me.

Halal and Kosher, Vegan and Vegetarian

While I have tried to make everything Halal and Kosher some of the recipes contain alcohol and a few contain gelatine. I am working on alternative versions of these recipes, and I will publish them as soon as I can. My advice here would be to simply skip these recipes in favour of those that you are permitted to eat, but again, don't be afraid to adapt what you see here.

It has so far proved too difficult to make any of the recipes vegan and I have decided to concentrate on solely plant-based desserts a little later when I can devote enough time to them.

Most of the recipes are vegetarian.

Equipment

All my recipes have been created and tested in my homes. Below is a list of useful equipment I have and some related advice. Most of this equipment is available from your average cook shop.

Chopping boards/pans/trays/knives: Kitchen essentials that I will assume you have already.

Maryse: A French name for a silicone spatula, I use a few of different sizes. It's not something you absolutely need but they make life a lot easier. You probably only want one.

Whisk: Choose one that's light, has thin wire and feels good in your hand, you will be using it a fair bit. Again, I have a few but you probably only want one.

Metal bowls: Pyrex would work as well but is far scarier when dropped. Make sure you get bowls that will fit snugly into your pans for when you use a Bain Marie. And make sure they're big enough for the recipe and some violent whisking!

Wooden spoons: Terribly useful for all kinds of things.

Metal spoon: One big one is all you need, and it is the best thing for folding, but a Maryse will do the trick too.

Digital scales: Most ingredients in the recipes require digital scales to weigh out. They don't have to be super expensive, but a tare (zero) button is a must.

Measuring spoons: These are used for things like salt, xanthan gum and spices that you only need small amounts of. All measurements given are in metric level spoons full.

Measuring jug: You want clearly defined increments and a spout that pours well. My jugs are mostly plastic and very cheap but work well.

Silicone moulds: Not things you absolutely need but I do use them in some recipes. There are alternatives you can use but these are very convenient.

Cranked Palette knife: I use a few different sizes, they're useful for smoothing/levelling the tops of things and lifting delicate things. I would suggest a blade of at least 5" but less than 10" (13-25cm). You don't want as many as I have, probably only one.

Pastry brush: Strangely enough this is for brushing pastry! I use old style fibre brushes rather than the newer silicone ones because I think they are better but use whatever you like!

Ice cream scoop: I have a few of slightly different sizes with handles that carry the heat from your hand to the ice cream. You probably don't need to spend that kind of money unless you are an ice cream addict like me! Get one that is solid, metal and will take some punishment as most frozen desserts will eventually destroy the scissor type scoops.

Microplane: Basically, a very fine grater that only takes the zest and not the pith of citrus fruits. Also, useful for grating nutmegs and chocolate.

Rolling pin. I have rather a lot of these in different sizes, all with flat ends so they're useful for bashing nuts etc. like in a pestle and mortar. I prefer wooden rolling pins, but I also own metal ones and plastic ones too. Use what you like best.

Sieves: You only really need a fine mesh sieve and one with larger holes. A few different sizes could be useful though, depending on the quantities you make, but not essential.

Coffee grinder: Very useful for grinding your sweetener/nuts but a food processor will probably do just as well.

Metal ring moulds: I use these for a few recipes that are too delicate for silicone moulds and for things I want to present nicely. I have a few in different shapes and sizes but basic small round ones are all you really need.

Tart rings: These rings have removable bases. I use 26cm rings with straight sides but use the fluted ones if you like. If you're a real pro you can use the ones with no base that I am used to, they need to go onto a very flat tray covered with silicone or greaseproof paper. This type of tart ring is a little less forgiving, but it does make a slightly better tart. Probably not worth the extra stress though.

Springform tins: These are only for cakes and can be substituted with older tins that don't come apart, they are however, very handy.

Silicone mats: Again, not necessary, but in the long run a lot cheaper than using lots of silicone or greaseproof paper. Don't buy any unless you cook a lot of desserts like me.

Ramekins: You will need these or something like them for a few of the recipes, they're heat proof and bounce rather well. Otherwise small cups or bowls will do at a pinch if they can take the heat of an oven.

Pastry cutters. You only need these for the odd recipe in this book, so don't bother buying them if you don't have any, and although they are pretty cheap, ring moulds will do the job just as well.

Parisienne scoop / melon baller: These are like very small ice cream scoops. They are very useful for making truffles the same size and round shape. You would only want one and preferably one that is not double ended, so you aren't constantly scooping the delicate palm of your hand as you use it.

Coeur a la crème mould: This heart shaped porcelain mould with several drainage holes in it is a niche piece of kit, but I really like mine. If you want, you can get the same effect by poking holes in a tin foil mould or tray, but tin foil is simply not as pretty!

Cooling rack: A simple wire cooling rack is very useful. I have recently seen nonstick ones in shops and in this Chef's opinion they are a superb waste of money. Cheap ones will last a very long time. Most that you see in professional kitchens are at least a decade old and still fine. They can also be used as a trivet for hot pans and such.

Blowtorch: You don't need a super powerful one of these. Essential for bursting those tiny little bubbles you get from whisking, as well as unmoulding things from metal ring moulds cleanly. I quite often use one to light gas ovens and the salamander at work, but you are unlikely to have that same need.

Stick blender: Just incredibly handy to have. It doesn't have to be super powerful, and these days you can get detachable ends with whisks on them and they can go in the dishwasher. I would honestly be lost without one.

Food processor: Not necessary, just useful, especially if you don't own a stick blender or coffee grinder. To be honest though, I only bought my first home one last year.

Mixer: If I wasn't writing this book, I certainly wouldn't have an orbital mixer, you can just do everything by hand, but they are good if you have to do larger quantities of things like whipped cream, meringue or pastry.

Oven: I have presented the oven temperatures in gas marks, Celsius and Fahrenheit for ease of use. I have tested the recipes in gas ovens and electric, with and without fans, and I don't think it makes much difference. I advise you to check the oven contents five minutes or more before the recipe says, to account for variation. Unless otherwise stated everything is cooked on the top shelf of a prewarmed oven.

Fridge-Freezer: I use an ordinary domestic fridge freezer with the fridge unit set to 2°c and the freezer underneath aiming for -18°c. I suggest you do the same. The top shelf of my fridge is kept for things to cool down on as heat rises and I don't want to affect the rest of my food.

Ice cream machine: My three basic ice cream recipes were designed with an ice cream machine in mind. I have made ice cream by hand on many occasions and it's not easy. If you are doing smaller quantities, then you could try the recipes by hand first as these machines are rather expensive. One of the models I have is over ten years old and still going strong. Mine have their own compressors, so no need to freeze the bowl. They were around £250 each and they still go for similar prices. A model like mine is rather overkill though, unless you have an ice cream addiction like I do.

Ingredients

Just so we're singing from the same hymn sheet, here is a list of ingredients I use in my recipes. They are all available from the three small supermarkets in my old town, nothing has come from the internet or a specialist food shop. You should therefore be able to get these ingredients easily enough in most parts of the UK, and indeed the world. I haven't done this because I'm afraid of the internet or anything, rather that in my experience most sugar free recipes for desserts contain weird products that I, as a professional Chef of twenty years, have never seen in the flesh. I wanted to make a book of recipes that are accessible for the average reader and that use fewer frightening substances. I have endeavoured to use as few unusual ingredients as possible, trying to stay true to the original recipes, their flavours, and their textures, but when I do use less common ingredients that is because they are needed.

Worth mentioning is my desire to keep things as low in carbohydrate and as cheap as possible too, so please shop around and find the best quality or price balance you can afford.

Truvia®: I'm using this as it is so widely available and is a standard strength. This sweetener is interchangeable with some other stevia and erythritol blends and I present a list of other substitutions at the back of the book. I know people prefer their own sweetener over others, so please feel free to substitute and experiment with the recipes to make them your own. People find this sweetener to have a mild laxative effect and I have found that one needs to consume rather a high quantity of any of the recipes to get these effects in any detrimental manner. Moderation may well be key.

Most of the recipes should be fairly open to an exchange of sweetener, especially if it is another stevia erythritol blend. For the ice creams it must be the stevia-erythritol type of the same strength or it will affect the hardness of the ice cream.

Cream: The cream in the recipes is double cream (55% fat), whipping cream (48% fat), and occasionally single cream (18% fat), all of which are supermarket own brand varieties.

Cacao: 100% chocolate isn't chocolate, it's Cacao. It's the lowest carb chocolate source available and is rather good quality. Substituting other dark chocolates of a lower percentage will affect the dish. The bigger the difference, the bigger the effect. I recently tried the ice cream recipe with a cheap 95% bar, and it was nothing like as nice as the original. 100% Cacao goes a long way and has a deep bitter flavour, as such I tend to use much less than traditional recipe ratios would suggest and many of my recipes still end up being seriously chocolatey. Please feel free to experiment.

Vanilla pods: These are important if you want true Vanilla flavour, the cured pod contains phenols and resins that contribute to true vanilla's complex flavour. Over two hundred compounds have been found in vanilla pods and you just don't get them with artificial vanilla essences, so paying a bit more for the real thing is worth it. Pods that have been scraped out but not used to infuse cream etc. can be put in a bottle of alcohol to extract as much of the valuable flavours as possible. I use Ndali® vanilla as it's the best I can find in a local supermarket. Ndali also do ground whole vanilla pods that work out to be way cheaper than the whole pods. Ndali produce is all ethical and the fair-trade standard is even based on them.

Vanilla extract: Extract, not essence! Extract is usually ground vanilla pods that weren't pretty enough for sale as is. You get many of the compounds you want and it's cheaper than the pods. I use this to bolster the more expensive vanilla pods or when I don't want the little black seeds everywhere. Essence is usually synthetic and has a very flat vanilla flavour.

Coffee: I'm using the best instant decaffeinated coffee I could buy locally for the recipes. Feel free to use ground coffee, just remember to adjust the recipe when adding liquids.

Flavour extracts and such: Very occasionally I use flavour extracts such as coconut, almond and mint. These are standard.

Butter: All butter in the recipes is unsalted. I buy middle of the road quality own brand butter usually, as the water content isn't so high as to affect recipes. The cheaper the butter the more water it contains.

Salt: I'm using cheap own brand table salt in most recipes, but feel free to use low sodium salt or pink Himalayan in its place. I do use more expensive sea salt flakes in my savoury home cooking, its lovely stuff and in my opinion worth splashing out for the occasional sprinkle.

Peanut butter, nut butters and tahini: I use Meridian foods nut and seed butters. They are the lowest carb variety I have found, and they are also free of palm oil, so no orangutan habitat has been destroyed for me to enjoy my desserts. Making your own is a worthwhile endeavor as you can control the carb count and limit nasty ingredients such as palm oil, but there isn't a great deal of a reason since it has already been done for you by experts. Several people may complain that peanuts are inflammatory. These recipes aren't for everyday use, and you can swap peanut butter for a nut butter if you like or just not eat it.

Coconut flour: I'm using the lowest carb type I could find. Beware, not all coconut flour is created equal, some has twice the carbs of others!

Gelatine: I use bronze strength leaf gelatine in my recipes. All leaf gelatine should gel the same amount of liquid per sheet, they just change the size of the sheet according to the strength. You can get this in tiny packs in supermarkets, but please buy cheaper larger quantities wherever you find it. Gelatine has the unique property of melting at body temperature, so desserts made with it tend to have much lighter characteristics than those using vegetarian alternatives like agar agar which will not melt once set. To use leaf gelatine just soak it in cold water for around five minutes, lift it out, give it a squeeze and add it to the recipe as directed.

ndali organic
vanilla powder

nature's

Xanthan gum: This stuff is so useful in so many ways. If it's in a recipe it's because it is needed, please try not to substitute it, gums and gels are not interchangeable. It is available in most supermarkets these days.

Glycerine: I know this one is a little contentious, but I've done a serious amount of research into glycerine, it's glycemic index and it's effects on blood glucose, insulin and ketosis. Glycerine, also known as glycerol, is a polyol, like erythritol etc. It has a very low glycemic index of only 3 making it half that of spinach. The point is that it is safe to use in low carb, ketogenic and diabetic diets.

Alcohol: Even in minute amounts it adds an interesting extra dimension to food, as we find foods containing it just a little exciting. All the alcohol in my recipes is cheap, own brand stuff from supermarkets. It can often be swapped for essences or alcohol-free versions. If you can find replacements, please feel free to experiment and improve on my recipes.

Citrus: All citrus fruits are unwaxed, average size and not organic.

Berries: These are fresh unless otherwise stated, some may even be from my garden. Frozen berries are interchangeable with fresh in many instances but certainly not all. The frozen type does have the benefit of being of a slightly more standardized and well checked carbohydrate count as well as the obvious longer-term storage benefits.

Nuts: All culinary nuts in these recipes are the cheapest ones I could get, so not organic or anything. I buy ground almonds in bags but otherwise all nuts are whole.

Coconut milk/cream: This is the kind you get in tins. I always go for the lowest carb stuff I can find, often that's the lower fat one and sometimes even the cheapest.

Nut milks: These are the unsweetened kind that you get in cartons. They need to be refrigerated like dairy milk but last a bit longer and are lower in those carbohydrates we're trying to dodge.

Spices: These are all cheap, own brand examples in little jars or packets. Buying smaller quantities is the idea here, as the oils will evaporate and leave you with tasteless powder over time. I grate my own nutmeg as it is particularly susceptible to this loss of oils but otherwise all spices are bought ground. But do feel free to travel to Zanzibar and grind your own, it is a magical place.

Pumpkin: I have used the tinned purée for all the recipe development for standardization, but feel free to use fresh pumpkin as a replacement. To make a purée you should deseed and roast the pumpkin flesh in a baking tray covered in foil. Cool the pumpkin once softened and scoop out the flesh with a spoon, then blitz in a food processor until smooth.

Agar agar: I use Agar crystal flakes rather than powdered stuff. Mostly because it is easier to weigh and measure in this form. This stuff is a vegan alternative to gelatine made from an algae, it is flavourless and apart from a high fibre content it has negligible nutritional value. To properly activate the gelation, it needs to be cooked in a liquid at a rolling boil for three minutes or more.

Rhubarb: I'm a very big fan of this stuff, and I have been eating home grown rhubarb since before I can remember. It is a strange vegetable that is usually grouped in with fruits, much the opposite of the tomato. All the rhubarb in these recipes is fresh and not the forced kind. Before use, you need to trim away the end that was attached to the "crown" and any parts where there is any leaf attached. The stalks then need to be washed thoroughly before cooking. Always remember to trim away the leaf, as it is quite poisonous.

Eggs: All eggs in the recipes are medium free-range eggs from supermarkets. Please feel free to buy free range eggs from smallholdings etc., the quality will be so much better, they will taste better, be more nutritious and are less likely to cost the earth. Supermarket eggs, however, are guaranteed to be inoculated against salmonella, unlike those from small farms etc.

Pasteurised liquid egg whites: I suggest using pasteurised egg whites in some mousse recipes where the egg won't be cooked. These can be found refrigerated and ready to use in cartons in supermarkets. I personally eat raw egg quite regularly, but I advise you not to do the same, especially if you might be pregnant or elderly, a child or already unwell.

Techniques

If you are new to cookery I encourage you to watch some videos and search the internet if you can rather than just relying on my clumsy words.

Possibly most important is your choice of music. I normally go with something good to sing along to, maybe even have a bit of a dance while you whisk. Be careful though, I once had to go to hospital after losing the end of my finger chopping tomatoes to Bon Jovi!

Bain Marie: Basically, you've got a saucepan of simmering water with a bowl over it, fitting snugly so the steam mostly stays in the pan. The water shouldn't touch the bowl, so the temperature being transferred to the bowl will never be above a hundred degrees Celsius. You need to use a heatproof bowl, so metal or Pyrex etc., or another saucepan that fits properly, but a bowl is better. This is useful for making custards as it is so gentle, but if you are attentive enough you can get away with just having a pan straight on the flame, it just means an awful lot of whisking.

Clingfilm trick: Normally when you roll out pastry the advice is to use the rolling pin and roll the pastry onto it to transfer it over to the tart ring etc. Without gluten the pastry used in these recipes is brittle. The thing to do is to roll out your pastry on a layer of clingfilm, once it is thin enough you can pick up the pastry by the clingfilm and gently flip it over the tart ring etc., poke the pastry into the corners and remove the clingfilm.

Folding: This technique is a way to combine ingredients without bursting many of the bubbles in them. Using a metal spoon gently make circular cutting motions through the components being mixed from the outside to the middle. This is a laborious task and often takes time, be patient, it's not something you should rush.

Water bath: Different from a Bain Marie, but similar. You put a tray in the oven with water in it and whatever you are cooking in the water. This makes the heat transference a lot gentler, so it's good for delicate desserts. The water should come about half the way up what you are cooking. I usually use water from the hot tap and put the water in once everything else is together in the oven, so you don't have to move a tray full of hot water around and spill it. A popular addition is a folded tea towel in the base of the water bath to further insulate the dessert you are cooking from any direct heat. Covering the whole thing with foil will give you an even gentler heat and the benefit of a little steam.

Custard: The test for custards being ready is that your finger will leave a trail on the back of a wooden spoon, and it will be viscous enough not to come back together.

Scalding: This one is simple, bringing liquids, usually dairy, to just under a boil and removing them from the heat. This can be important as it changes the proteins and fat globule size, making the liquids set better later, or combine better with other ingredients, like chocolate.

Churning: Ice cream machines churn the custard or syrup as it freezes to keep the ice crystals as small as possible. If you don't have an ice cream machine you can do it by hand. Get the largest bowl that will fit in your freezer and a sturdy whisk. You need to take the bowl out of the freezer every half hour or so and churn the ice cream by hand. This can take a long time if you're making a lot. Once I spent a whole day churning ice cream at a friend's flat and it was really, really tiring! The idea is to break up the ice crystals as much as possible and this takes some hard work.

Passing: This is simply forcing something through a sieve to remove unwanted solid parts like seeds. There is a lot of this in professional kitchens and in this book, usually with the finest sieve you can find. With the volumes Chefs deal with we use a ladle, but you will only need to use the back of a spoon.

Cartouche: A disc of baking parchment or the like that is made by folding the paper repeatedly in the way that one would make a paper snowflake decoration. Fold your paper to bring one edge against another and form a triangle. Trim any excess. Fold the paper again to bring the two furthest corners of the new diagonal fold together. You have now got one corner that has been the axis that all these folds have had in common, and if you unfold the paper at this stage you will find that this point is in the middle of the paper. Keeping that one corner towards you, fold the two long edges together until you don't feel you can fold the paper anymore, or at least five times, and trim the cartouche to the correct size: Take the point which will become the center of the circle and place it in the middle of the tart ring etc. that it is to fit. Take a pair of scissors and cut the paper to the radius of the tart ring. When you unfold the paper, you should have a rough circle.

Another method is to cut out a rough circle of parchment and crumple it then flatten it out or to simply draw a pencil circle on the paper with the ring as a guide and cut that out.

A cartouche can be used as a lid for things that you don't want to cook in much water or that you want to cook quickly. Or of course if you simply can't find that saucepan's lid. This technique allows for evaporation without the forming of a "skin", and the original cheffy method does mean that you can cut a hole in the center of the disc which allows even faster evaporation.

Heating a knife: A hot sharp knife is useful for cutting lots of things in the world of patisserie. To heat your knife, place the blade, tip downwards in a jug or other container of hot water for a minute or so. Wipe it dry and cut with it. Clean the blade before returning it to the water to heat up for the next cut.

Chocolate bavarois

Serves four

Once as a Commis Chef I tipped over a whole tray of chocolate bavarois while I attempted to clean the walk-in fridge. Unfortunately, chocolate bavarois always remind me of that moment, but it's not so bad, because I got to eat the small amount that wasn't flung across the floor!

1 leaf of gelatine

200g of whipping cream

2 egg yolks

45g sweetener

45g cacao

A pinch of salt

100g whipping cream

Soften the gelatine in enough cold water to cover it for about five minutes.

Place the salt, sweetener and 100g of the cream in a saucepan to scald and remove from the heat.

After cooling for a minute or so, whisk the yolks into the saucepan. Return to a low heat, whisking until thickened, and remove from the heat again.

Break up the cacao and add to the custard.

Squeeze any water from the gelatine and add it to the custard.

Mix the cacao and gelatine into the custard with a thin metal spoon.

Whip 200g of your cream to soft peaks and fold into the custard mix with the metal spoon a third at a time.

Once the mixture is uniformly mixed, spoon it into lightly oiled ring moulds with a base of foil or clingfilm.

To unmould, remove the clingfilm or foil and place the mould on a plate. Lightly heat the mould with a blowtorch until the ring simply slides off.

Vanilla bavarois

Serves five

Bavarois or Crème Bavaroise is one of the reasons staff retention in the hospitality industry isn't worse than it already is: When food like this is available it can be hard to make that move into acting!

3 leaves of gelatine

150g double cream

300g water

90g sweetener

1 vanilla pod, split and seeds scraped

1 tsp vanilla extract

3 egg yolks

300g whipping cream, whipped to soft peaks

To lower the fat, the double cream can be exchanged for whipping cream.

Combine the double cream, vanilla, sweetener and water in a saucepan and bring up to almost boiling before removing from the heat.

Soften the gelatine in enough cold water to cover it for about five minutes.

After a minute to cool, whisk a little of the cream mixture into the egg yolks to temper them.

Whisk the egg yolk mix into the slightly cooled vanilla liquid and return to a very gentle heat, whisking until the custard is thickened enough to cover the back of a wooden spoon.

Squeeze the water from the gelatine and add the softened leaves to your custard.

Pass the custard through a fine sieve and put it aside or chill, stirring occasionally until it is cool and to starts to form a skin on the surface.

Whip the remaining cream to soft peaks.

Gently fold your softly whipped cream into the crème anglaise collée (the custard) in three batches and transfer to glasses, small bowls or lightly oiled moulds.

Chill in the fridge for eight hours or overnight.

Variations on a bavarois

For a coffee bavarois, simply exchange the vanilla in the original recipe for 2 ½ tsp of good quality instant coffee and proceed as normal.

For a fruit bavarois, remove the vanilla from the original recipe and exchange the water with the same weight of seedless berry or passion fruit puree. The quantities of sweetener will have to be changed to taste according to the ripeness and tartness of the fruits used. This will also work with sieved rhubarb.

And for coconut bavarois, remove the vanilla from the original recipe. Exchange the double cream and water for coconut cream and coconut milk and add 2 tsp coconut essence. Otherwise proceed as usual.

Blancmange

Serves four

The medieval period tends to conjure romantic feelings in some. The reality however would have been quite ghastly by our standards, especially the food. For example, a dessert called leach was made with honey, milk and the gelatine from the swim bladders of certain fish. Not the finest of flavours I'm sure. Modern blancmange has survived those dark ages and is thankfully not flavoured with trout.

200g unsweetened almond milk

200g whipping cream

40g sweetener

½ a vanilla pod, split and seeds scraped out

¼ tsp xanthan

¼ tsp agar agar crystals

¼ tsp lemon juice

A pinch of salt

Whisk all the ingredients together in a small saucepan.

Bring the whole lot up to a simmer for 5 minutes, whisking occasionally.

Remove from the heat.

Lightly pass the flame of a blowtorch over the surface of the mixture to burst any bubbles.

Pass the liquid through a sieve to remove the vanilla pod.

Pour into ramekins and repeat the use of the blowtorch if any bubbles remain.

Chill for at least 6 hours.

Walnut blondies

Serves nine

I used to think brownies were just a bit of cake, but when I finally embraced their gooeyness, I discovered a world of possibilities which neatly arrived at blondies. In my opinion these brownies' cousins are even harder to execute well than their darker relatives, especially without such things as white chocolate or sugar, and so outcome the big guns in the form of delicious brown butter!!

180g butter

180g peanut butter

2 tsp baking powder

2 tsp vanilla extract

60g ground almonds

3 eggs

30g cocoa nibs

¼ tsp xanthan

45g sweetener

60g clotted cream

60g walnuts, crushed

Weigh out the butter into a small saucepan and gently heat until melted and foaming.

Once foamy, swirl the pan a little to check the colour of the milk solids that by now should have collected at the bottom.

Keep checking the milk solids in this way every ten seconds or so.

Around the same time that the foaming subsides a little you should notice a nutty smell and upon swirling the butter you will notice that the milk solids have begun to brown.

Remove the saucepan from the heat and continue to gently swirl the pan for around a minute.

Leave the brown butter to cool a little while you preheat your oven to 140°c / gas mark 1 / 275°f.

Mix all the other ingredients together and beat well to incorporate some air.

Line a 9" square baking tin with parchment paper.

Mix the brown butter into the rest of the batter, trying to save every bit of the browned milk solids from the saucepan.

Give the mixture a good beat until a pleasing uniformity is reached.

Spoon the mix into the lined tin and smooth the top a little.

Bake for 35 minutes.

Allow to cool for an hour and then chill overnight in a fridge.

Cut into nine squares and microwave for 30 seconds to serve.

Chocolate brownies

Serves nine

As I said, for years I was resistant to having brownies on the menus where I worked. I saw it as just a bit of chocolate sponge, not restaurant food. As it turned out I had been eating substandard brownies all that time, so I hadn't understood. Brownies for me must be chocolatey, dense, gungy squares of delicious excess. The kind of thing you want to eat alone because of the mess you make and that look you get on your face.

200g cacao

200g butter

6 eggs

4 egg whites (120g)

120g sweetener

150g hazelnuts, roasted & ground

40g coconut flour

2 tsp baking powder

½ tsp xanthan

A pinch of salt

Line a 9" square baking tin with parchment.

To make a ganache, melt the cacao and butter together in a small saucepan or Bain Marie and remove from the heat to cool.

Meanwhile beat the egg whites to stiff peaks, first adding the salt and then the sweetener once nice and fluffy.

Preheat your oven to 165°c / gas mark 3 / 325°f.

Crack and whisk the whole eggs and incorporate into the slightly cooled ganache.

Give the egg whites a final mix and fold them into the chocolate mixture in three parts.

When the last third of beaten egg white is only just incorporated, add the rest of the ingredients and fold them in to create a harmonious mixture.

Gently spoon the mix into the lined tin and smooth the top a little.

Bake for 20 minutes.

The brownie should be dull and cake-like around the edges but shiny and mousse-like in the middle with quite a wobble when tapped.

Allow to cool for an hour and then chill overnight in a fridge.

Cut into nine portions in the tin, turn them out, and remove the parchment.

Microwave the portions on full power for 30 seconds, warm through a low oven, or serve cold.

Lemon cheesecake

Serves three

I grew up with cheesecakes that came out of packets: add milk and whisk etc. Later I enjoyed simple non-baked cheesecakes and later the baked kind. This recipe is the unbaked kind with just a touch of gelatine. Honestly this kind of cheesecake is still my favourite, it's simple and quick to make, and I'm a really big fan of that silky texture. Hopefully it is that texture that makes me most keen on this type, or I might just be a bit lazy!

30g butter, softened

30g ground almonds

40g coconut flour

1 leaf of gelatine

1 lemon, zest and juice

45g sweetener

250g cream cheese

100g whipping cream

Tightly cover the bottoms of three ring moulds with clingfilm. I usually go with a double layer.

Combine the ingredients for the base and press into the bottom of the moulds. You can use your fingers, but I prefer the back of a spoon. If I was making a large cheesecake, I would go all the way up the sides, but for individual ones, just the base will do.

Soften the gelatine in enough cold water to cover it for about five minutes.

Meanwhile combine the zest, juice and sweetener in a microwave safe bowl and heat up to just above body temperature.

Once soft, squeeze the water from the gelatine, and add it to the lemon mix, stirring to combine.

Whip your cream to soft peaks, fold a little through the lemon mix and then fold that back through the cream.

Soften the cream cheese with a spoon until it is smooth and fold the cream and lemon mix through the cream cheese.

Add the mixture into your ring moulds on top of the almond base.

Tap the mould with a spoon to settle the mixture.

Chill in the fridge for at least four hours or more.

To unmould, remove the clingfilm and, place the cheesecake on a plate. Gently warm the rings with a blowtorch just enough to loosen the cheesecake from the sides. The ring should simply slide off.

Variations on a Lemon cheesecake

Most citrus fruits will replace the lemon very well, chiefly blood orange, lime or yuzu.

Coffee makes a good cheesecake. Simply omit the citrus and use 2 tbsp of espresso (or very strong instant coffee) in the place of the lemon juice.

For blueberry cheesecake replace the citrus with 2 tbsp of water and ½ tsp of good vanilla extract. Then just add washed blueberries to each cheesecake as you fill the moulds. I would go with around 10g per portion. Lightly roasting the berries will soften them if you prefer them that way.

Strawberry, raspberry and blackberry cheesecakes are achieved in much the same way as the blueberry cheesecakes mentioned above, but they will need to be chopped up a little!

For Stracciatella cheesecake, just replace the lemon with 2 tbsp of water and ½ tsp of vanilla extract. Then simply add 25g cacao nibs to the mix during the final folding and fill the moulds as normal.

Baked cheesecake

Serves twelve

Cheesecake is rather a silly name for this. It isn't a cake and cream cheese isn't the first thing you think of when someone mentions cheese. Cream cheese tart could be a better label but then you might think it was in pastry. Cream cheese flan just isn't good enough. It's certainly not a pie either. I suppose it might be a torte. Hmmm. At least it does get baked!

120g butter, softened

120g ground almonds

160g coconut flour

600g cream cheese

300g soured cream

65g sweetener

4 eggs

1 ½ tsp vanilla extract

Zest of a lemon

Preheat your oven to 165°c / gas mark 3 / 325°f.

Combine the ingredients for the base and press into a 20cm springform tin lined with greaseproof paper. You can use your fingers, but I prefer the back of a spoon. You can push the base all the way up the sides, halfway up or just on the base, it's up to you but I go all the way up usually.

Bake the base for 10 minutes.

Remove the base to cool somewhere while you make the filling.

Whisk the eggs, incorporate the soured cream, then the cream cheese and the rest of the ingredients.

Turn your oven down to 140°c / gas mark 1 / 275°f and bake for 1 hour.

There should be a slight wobble in the centre, and the top will likely be slightly coloured.

Remove to somewhere the cheesecake can cool for an hour and then chill in your fridge for at least eight hours, or overnight.

A hot clean knife would be best for cutting this.

To lower the fat content, replace the cream cheese with the low fat variety. If you want to lower the fat even further, then you can always swap the soured cream for a low fat crème fraiche or even yoghurt.

Variations on a baked cheesecake

Some simple and common variations would be to stir cacao nibs, (sugar free) chocolate chips, or blueberries through the filling. You would want to omit the lemon if you added the chocolate.

Swapping the lemon zest for lime zest makes a nice change too.

If you want a coffee cheesecake, simply omit the vanilla and lemon zest and replace it with two teaspoons of good quality powdered instant coffee dissolved into 2 tsp of water or the same amount of espresso.

Blueberry cobbler

Serves eight

There are several different schools of thought on how to do this dish, but I like it to look like the cobble stones of an old street, thinking that perhaps that is where the name came from. I like small roundish cobbles rather than large "flagstones" which would have made for a terrible name. A fair bit better than blueberry tarmac though.

150g ground almonds

100g coconut flour

100g butter, softened

100g double cream

4 eggs

125g sweetener

4 tsp baking powder

1 tsp xanthan

2 tsp vanilla extract

A pinch of salt

500g blueberries

85g sweetener

100g water

A pinch of xanthan

Mix all the ingredients for the topping, until a uniform mixture is formed.

Mix all the ingredients for the fruit base in whatever vessel you are going to use for the cobbler. Spread the contents evenly across the base of the dish.

Preheat your oven to 165°c / gas mark 3 / 325°f.

Roll out the dough between to sheets of greaseproof paper, to about a 1cm thickness. Transfer the dough to the freezer or fridge if you don't have freezer space.

Once it has firmed up use a cutter to cut out rounds or any other shape, and carefully transfer them onto the top of the fruit mixture. Leave a little overlap from each cobble to the next and some space for the contents to ooze.

Bake for 25 minutes.

Variations on a cobbler

A simple addition to the blueberries is the zest of one or two limes.

For a blackberry cobbler, replace the blueberries with blackberries and reduce the sweetener to 75g. Otherwise proceed in the same way.

For a rhubarb and orange cobbler, peel, segment and dice an orange and add it to 500g of washed rhubarb cut into 1 inch lengths. Use this in place of the blueberries and reduce the sweetener to 65g. Otherwise proceed normally.

Coeur a la crème

Serves four

Literally translated this means "heart of cream", which is what it is. If you referred to it in English though it would sound misleadingly boring. The reality of this dessert is so simply delicious that you must use its French nomenclature just to do it justice, unless of course you are French, in which case it sounds pretty boring no matter what you call it.

400g cream cheese

400g crème fraiche

50g sweetener

30g lemon juice (1 lemon)

1 tsp vanilla extract

A pinch of salt

You will need a Coeur a la crème mould for each person, and a square of muslin and something to weight each mould down with.

Alternatively, a foil container with some holes poked in the base will serve as a much cheaper mould.

Combine all the ingredients and beat well.

Line your moulds with muslin cloth and divide the creamy mixture equally among them.

Fold the muslin cloth over the tops of the cream mix and weigh the contents down with something no more than double the weight of the dessert itself.

Chill for at least eight hours or overnight.

To serve, remove the weight and peel away the muslin, then invert the mould onto a serving plate and lift the mould & cloth cleanly away.

Variations on a Coeur a la crème

I have done this dessert with several different brands and forms of cream cheeses: mascarpone, ricotta and quark and the dish has worked perfectly each time.

Crema Gianduja

Serves four

The Napoleonic wars had some surprising culinary effects, one of which was the creation of a chocolate and hazelnut paste by beleaguered Italians. Necessity really is the mother of invention sometimes, and Napoleon might just be the mother of Nutella!

150g hazelnut butter

85g butter

25g sweetener

180g double cream

15g cacao, broken up

Bring all the ingredients except the cacao, up to a simmer and remove from the heat.

Drop the cacao into the hot mixture and stir a few times until a smooth even distribution is accomplished.

Gently pour the mix into ramekins, glasses or whatever you intend to serve it in.

Chill in the fridge for at least eight hours or overnight.

Crème collée

Serves four

This translates as glued cream, which doesn't sound very attractive. The other way it is known in French is Crème à la gelatine, which means gelatine cream, and might be even less attractive than the first name. It just goes to show how much better things sound in French and explains a little why menus were written in that way for so long!

2 sheets of gelatine

550g single cream

35g sweetener

1 vanilla pod, seeds scraped & removed

4 egg yolks

1 egg

Soak the gelatine in as much cold water as it takes to cover it.

Bring the cream, sweetener and vanilla up to just under boiling point in a small saucepan and remove from the heat.

After a minute, whisk the egg and egg yolks together.

Whisk a little of the sweetened cream into the eggs, then whisk that back into the rest of the cream mixture.

Return the pan to a gentle heat and whisk continuously until the custard thickens enough to coat the back of a wooden spoon, then remove from the heat.

Squeeze any excess water from the softened gelatine leaves and add them to the custard, stirring to combine.

Pass the liquid through a fine sieve and pour into serving glasses, ramekins or something similar.

Briefly pass the flame of a blowtorch across the surface of the custards to burst any bubbles.

Chill the custards in a fridge for eight hours or more.

Lemon and almond cremeaux

Serves three

Naming things a cremeaux used to really annoy me because it is a verb rather than a noun, a description rather than a name. Obviously, I got over it. Calling it lemon and almond creamy is far better than lemon and almond stuff anyway.

400g single cream

1 lemon juice & zest

50g sweetener

3 egg yolks

200g almond butter

Bring the cream, sweetener and lemon up to boiling point and remove it from the heat.

After a minute to cool, press the hot liquid through a fine sieve.

Whisk a little of the hot cream mix onto the egg yolks to temper them.

Whisk the tempered egg yolk back into the cream mixture and return the saucepan to a gentle heat.

Whisk the custard continuously until it thickens enough to coat the back of a wooden spoon.

Remove from the heat and stir in the almond butter until fully combined.

Pass through a fine sieve and divide amongst ramekins, glasses, bowls etc.

Chill in a fridge for eight hours or overnight.

Variations on a cremeaux

Replacing the almond butter with other nut or seed butters works very well.

My suggestions are hazelnut butter, peanut butter and tahini.

Crumble

Serves four

As a Chef I get asked what my favourite food is, and I normally say custard, because I'm cheeky, and "custard" covers such a wide range of dishes that you might never get bored. The same is true of crumbles. There are so many different variations you could have in your crumble from one day to the next that you could never tire of eating one. Of course, what I should probably say is crumble and custard if I can get away with it, because that's a whole lot of deliciousness, and, because I'm cheeky.

For the crumble....

300g ground almonds

70g butter, soft

25g sweetener

A pinch of salt

A few options for the base

Rhubarb crumble

300g rhubarb

40g sweetener

Strawberry and rhubarb crumble

150g strawberries, hulled

150g rhubarb

20g sweetener

Blackberry crumble

300g blackberries

10g sweetener

Place all the ingredients for the crumble topping in a bowl and loosely rub them together with your hands.

Set the bowl aside in the fridge.

Preheat your oven to 177°c / gas mark 4 / 350°f.

Slice the fruit for the base and gently mix with the sweetener.

Divide the fruit amongst ramekins or a large ovenproof dish.

Crumble the almond mixture onto the fruit base as lightly as possible with your fingertips.

Bake for 20 minutes.

Remove the crumbles from the oven and serve.

Variations on a crumble

Other nuts and seeds can be used in the crumble topping instead of almonds.

To make the crumbles vegan, coconut oil or nut butters can be used in place of the butter.

Black currant fool

Serves eight

The flavour of blackcurrants is incredible, which is why I'm surprised that they aren't more widely used. If you consider the level of vitamin C, the fibre and the abundant anthocyanins in the fruits, they make this cream laden dessert into health food (If you ignore the cream).

150g black currants

25g sweetener

2 tbsp kirsch

100g black currants

25g sweetener

1 tbsp kirsch

100g red wine

900g whipping cream

Heat the first set of ingredients in a saucepan and boil for a minute.

Leave to cool for ten minutes, mash with a fork and refrigerate.

Heat the second set of ingredients until nearly all the kirsch has boiled off. Push the fruit through a fine sieve to obtain a purée and chill.

Whip the cream to soft peaks.

Roughly stir the mashed fruit through the cream.

Layer the fruit cream and purée in glasses.

Variations on a black currant fool

Red or white currants will work in place of the black currants as will most berries, but the sweetener levels will have to be adjusted.

Lemon fool

Serves three

My mother does fruit fools two ways, one with a fruit purée, whipped cream and custard, and the other just with fruit and cream. I have always thought of the one with custard as being the proper way. This recipe doesn't have a fruit purée, but you could call the lemony part a custard, if you like.

100g double cream

2 lemon's juice

½ lemon's zest

40g sweetener

3 egg yolks

200g double cream

Boil the first set of ingredients except the egg, for 3 minutes and remove from the heat while you separate the eggs.

Temper the egg with a little of the lemon cream and mix them through the rest of the cream.

Whisk until thick enough to coat the back of a wooden spoon.

Remove from the heat to cool for ten minutes before chilling in the fridge for at least an hour.

Whip the remaining cream to stiff peaks.

Slacken the whipped cream with a third of the cold lemon custard and whip it back up.

Slacken with another third and rewhip.

Slacken and rewhip again with the remaining lemon custard.

Transfer to serving glasses, ramekins, or whatever you intend to use and chill in a fridge for at least four hours.

Passionfruit fool

Serves four

Fruit fools are something I grew up with. They were normally made from the damsons we had growing in our garden, foraged blackberries, or sometimes rhubarb, also from our garden. I am sure that if my mother could have grown passion fruit, they would have graced our table just as often if not more.

100g butter

25g sweetener

30g passion fruit pulp, sieved

3 egg yolks

300g whipping cream

60g passion fruit pulp, including seeds

Combine the butter and sweetener in a small saucepan and gently heat until the butter has melted.

Remove the pan from the heat and add the passion fruit pulp, stirring to combine.

After cooling for a minute or so, temper the egg yolks by whisking a little of the warm fruit and butter mix into them.

Whisk the tempered egg yolk mixture back into the saucepan and return to a very gentle heat.

Whisk the mixture until it begins to thicken and immediately remove from the heat.

Continue to whisk the mixture as it cools for a minute and transfer to a fridge to chill.

Whip the cream until stiff peaks form when the whisk is removed.

Fold the passion fruit pulp and seeds through the cream.

Partially fold the passion fruit curd through the cream mixture, leaving streaks of more concentrated flavour.

Layer the cream mixture in serving glasses with occasional blobs of the remaining curd.

Red fruit jelly

Serves two

Jelly is great. Jelly and ice cream is really great. What I think is really, really great are the big wobbly jellies made in old school jelly moulds. Over the years I've made castle shaped jellies, fish shaped jellies, rabbit shaped jellies and all manner of weirdly shaped jellies with French names like barquette. Of course, you can just set it in a glass and put a blob of cream on top.

50g raspberries

50g strawberries

200g water

15g sweetener

1 leaf of gelatine

Soak the gelatine leaf in as much cold water as it takes to cover it, for around five minutes.

Place all the remaining ingredients in a small saucepan and bring up to a boil.

When it reaches boiling point remove the pan from the heat.

Pass the fruit and liquid through a fine sieve.

Squeeze out any excess water from the softened gelatine leaf and add it to the hot liquid.

After a minute, give the liquid a good stir.

Leave the hot liquid to cool for five minutes and gently stir.

Gently pass the flame of a blowtorch across the surface of the liquid to burst any bubbles.

Transfer the liquid to moulds or glasses.

Repeat the action with the blowtorch if any bubbles remain.

Chill the jellies for 8 hours or overnight.

To unmould dip the mould in very hot water briefly to slightly melt the outside of the jelly.

Invert the jelly mould on your serving plate and jiggle it until the jelly slips out.

Moelleux au chocolat

Serves five

This isn't a chocolate fondant, this is a hot, moussey, chocolate cake with a center of liquid ganache. I believe it is also known as a lava cake, but everything sounds a little bit classier in French. Right?

200 double cream

200g butter

30g sweetener

50g cacao, broken up

⅛ tsp xanthan

100g cacao

80g butter

30g ground almonds

75g sweetener

3 eggs, separated

Bring the cream, butter and sweetener from the first list to just under boiling point and remove from the heat.

Stir in the cacao until fully combined.

Stir in the xanthan gum.

Pass the ganache through a fine sieve.

Chill in a fridge until set.

Put the cacao, butter and sweetener from the second list in a bain-marie and melt, until a nice liquid mixture is formed.

Divide the ganache into five equal lumps and place them in the center of each of your ramekins.

Heat your oven to 200°c / gas mark 6 / 400°f.

Remove the bowl of chocolate mixture from the heat to cool and add the almonds, stirring until fully combined.

Beat the egg whites until stiff peaks form when you remove the whisk.

Mix the egg yolks through the chocolate and almond mixture.

Fold the egg whites into the chocolate mix one third at a time.

Gently spoon into the ramekins, over the ganache blob.

Arrange on a baking tray and bake for exactly 14 minutes.

Baked chocolate mousse

Serves six

I first saw a baked chocolate mousse in Claire Clarke's beautiful book "Indulge". A modified version of it was once called "better than sex" by one of my customers. Obviously, all the credit for that goes to Claire. This recipe is rather a departure from that one but remains heavily inspired by the original.

90g 100% cacao, broken up

190g double cream

80g sweetener

¼ tsp xanthan

3 egg whites

A pinch of salt

Scald the cream, sweetener and salt, and remove from the heat.

Add the xanthan gum and give a good whisk.

Add the cacao and wait a good minute for it to melt a bit.

During this spare minute you can pre heat your oven to 165°c / gas 3 / 325°f.

Whisk the mixture again, wait another minute and give it a final mix.

During that spare minute you can tinfoil the bases of some metal ring moulds. Bear in mind that this will need to be done rather securely to stop the mousse evacuating.

Once the chocolate cream has cooled to just above body temperature whisk the egg whites to soft peaks and fold through the chocolate cream in three batches.

Pour your mousse equally into six moulds and place in the oven for 7 minutes.

Remove the mousses to cool and chill overnight in the fridge.

To unmould simply peel off the foil and warm the ring mould with a blowtorch slightly. The mousses will slide out.

Buttermilk mousse

Serves four

I first saw a recipe like this when I was freelancing for a friend one summer in the Cotswolds. I really liked the simplicity of it, so when my tenure with him was over I came up with my own take on it. I won't mention who he is though, because he's got a big enough head already!

300g live cultured buttermilk

200g double cream

55g sweetener

A pinch of salt

2 sheets of gelatine

Soak the gelatine in enough cold water to cover it for about five minutes.

Bring half the cream, the sweetener and the salt up to scalding point and remove from the heat.

Squeeze any excess water from the gelatine and add it to the hot cream.

After a minute give the hot liquid a good stir to ensure that the gelatine has dissolved.

Whip the rest of the cream to soft peaks.

Mix the buttermilk into the slightly cooled cream mixture and fold in the cream in two batches.

Gently transfer the dessert into glasses or similar.

Chill in a fridge for at least four hours.

Chocolate mousse

Serves four

When I was head Chef in New Zealand my predecessor had made such bad chocolate mousses that I couldn't put my own on the menu, even years after I had taken over. It really isn't hard to make a basic chocolate mousse and make it delicious, so I can only imagine what was stopping him back then! Perhaps it was that he didn't have this recipe?

40g cacao, broken up

200g whipping cream

30g sweetener

90g pasteurized egg whites

Scald the cream with the sweetener and remove from the heat.

Stir in the cacao until combined.

Whisk the egg whites until soft peaks are formed and fold into the chocolate mixture in three batches.

As soon as the egg white is evenly mixed, transfer the mousse to glasses, bowls or whatever takes your fancy.

Chill for at least four hours.

Chocolate orange mousse

Serves four

Chocolate and orange is one of those great flavour combinations that it is difficult to have too much of. I recently experimented extensively in this area, and found that the limitations of time, work and the wallet were all that could effectively limit my indulgence. Of course, to be properly scientific all experiments need to be repeated several times. For science.

140g double cream

1 Orange, zest and 50g juice

10g orange flower water

20g sweetener

40g cacao, broken up

75g pasteurized egg whites

Place the orange flower water and the sweetener in a small saucepan with the finely grated zest and the juice of the orange.

Add the cream to the saucepan and bring the contents to gentle simmer for 3 minutes then remove from the heat.

Strain the cream and orange mixture through a fine sieve into a bowl containing the cacao.

Stir in the cacao until combined.

Leave the mixture too cool for 10 minutes.

Whisk the egg whites until soft peaks are formed and fold into the chocolate mixture in three batches.

As soon as the egg white is evenly mixed, transfer the mousse to glasses, ramekins or similar.

Chill for at least four hours.

Coffee mousse

Serves two

I wrote this recipe for use in a roulade at a friend's request, but it works equally well on its own, or as part of a layered verrine. It would work especially well alone in a dark place with a spoon and naughty look on your face.

2 leaf gelatine

3 tsp good instant coffee

2 tbsp boiled water

25g sweetener

300g whipping cream, whipped to stiff peaks

Soften the gelatine in cold water for around five minutes.

Combine the coffee, water and sweetener in a bowl or similar and add the softened gelatine.

Once the coffee mixture is a little cooler mix a little of the cream through it and then fold that carefully back through the cream.

Set in moulds, pipe it whilst still soft or whatever you want to do with it.

Hazelnut mousse

Serves eight

One of the annoying things about a mousse set with gelatine is the time waiting for it to gel. In a professional kitchen you make a lot of things the day before or in the early morning and there's never enough time to find yourself waiting. It's a little different at home, so I wonder what you will do in those four hours. You could go for a walk, read a book or learn a new skill. Just please don't start writing a book of low carb dessert recipes. Please.

300g hazelnut butter

200g hazelnuts toasted and ground

100g walnut oil

1 tsp cocoa powder

2 sheets of gelatine

75g sweetener

30g lemon juice (1 lemon)

2 tsp brandy

400g whipping cream

Soak the gelatine in enough cold water to cover it for about five minutes.

Combine the oil, hazelnut and cocoa in a bowl and mix thoroughly.

Warm the lemon juice and brandy with the sweetener until just simmering and remove from the heat.

Squeeze any excess water from the gelatine leaves and add them to the hot liquid in the saucepan.

Whip the cream to stiff peaks.

Stir a tablespoon of the cream through the warm liquid in the saucepan and then fold that back through the whipped cream.

Fold the nut mixture through the cream.

As soon as the mousse ingredients are all uniformly distributed throughout, transfer the mixture into serving glasses.

Chill for at least four hours.

Passion fruit mousse

Serves four

One of the treats of the winter is the abundance of citrus fruits and passion fruit. Of course, passion fruit are available much longer than just winter, but they are a last vestige of vibrancy and exotic verve in a depressing climate that can be all that is needed to lift the mood. I have ended up with a great many passion fruit recipes over the years and I never tire of using the wrinkly little chaps, even if they may be rather annoying to prepare.

2 leaves of gelatine

6 passion fruit

15g sweetener

30g lemon juice (1 lemon)

300g whipping cream

Soak the gelatine leaves in enough water to cover them for about five minutes.

Halve the passion fruit and remove all the seeds and juice you can.

Strain the seeds through a rough sieve with the back of a spoon into a small saucepan.

Add the lemon juice and sweetener to the passion fruit pulp and heat until the sweetener has just dissolved.

Squeeze any excess water from the gelatine leaves and add to the hot fruit mixture, then set aside to cool slightly.

Whisk the cream to stiff peaks.

Take a tablespoon of the cream and stir it through the warm fruit mix, then fold that mixture back through the whipped cream.

Transfer to glasses etc. and chill for at least four hours.

Walnut mousse

Serves three

I have great memories of collecting the walnuts from a mighty tree in New Zealand every season. Gathering the walnuts, removing the weird husk and attempting to get the edible part out in two complete halves. I'm not sure how many intact halves I got in all those years, but let me tell you, the sense of triumph is elating and it's far less painful than shelling macadamias with a hammer!

1 sheet of gelatine

200g whipping cream

50g single cream

30g sweetener

10g lemon juice

200g walnuts, roasted & ground

120g walnut oil

Soak the gelatine in as much cold water as it takes to cover it for about five minutes, or until it softens.

Whip the whipping cream to soft peaks and set aside, at room temperature.

Warm the single cream with the sweetener and lemon juice until just under a boil and remove from the heat.

Squeeze any excess water from the gelatine and add it to the hot cream mixture, stirring until combined.

Fold the ground walnuts and walnut oil through the cream.

Take a spoonful of the whipped cream and mix it through the hot cream so they are closer to the same temperature.

Gently fold the cream and gelatine mix through the whipped cream.

Divide the mousse into serving glasses, or whatever you like and chill for four hours or more.

Variations on a walnut mousse

Exchange the walnuts for other nuts using the same quantities.

Panna cotta

Serves three

This Italian dessert is supposed to wobble suggestively, being only barely set by the gelatine. I gave up ordering these in restaurants years ago as they were invariably as sad and solid as a rubber ball and just as bouncy. I always craved a waitress's approach and that gentle wiggle that caused such sensuous anticipation, but I was instead met with a cold, unyielding blob! The recipe I give here is for a dessert so wobbly, so soft and so delicately balanced on the edge of being a liquid that you will never want to order one in a restaurant again either. For that I am most deeply sorry.

1 leaf of gelatine

35g sweetener

350g whipping cream

½ vanilla pod

Soften the gelatine in enough cold water to cover it for about five minutes.

While the gelatine "blooms", scald the cream with the sweetener and vanilla bean. The bean should be split lengthways and have the seeds scraped out, into the cream.

Remove the cream from the heat and add the softened gelatine. After around thirty seconds give the mix a good stir and pass through a fine sieve.

Pour into ramekins, dariole moulds or something similar.

Chill for at least 6 hours.

To unmold fill a pan, dish or similar with enough just boiled water to come ¾ of the way up the side of whatever the panna cotta has been set in.

After about 15 seconds invert the panna cotta onto a plate and it should slide out of your mould.

If it won't slide out at this stage just pop it back in the water for another five seconds and repeat.

Limit the time the panna cotta spends in the water as much as possible as it will melt very easily.

To lower the fat, you can substitute half of the cream with milk.

Variations on panna cotta

Saffron panna cotta

Use the same recipe and method as with the vanilla panna cotta but swap the vanilla for half a gram of saffron, let it infuse the cold liquid for thirty minutes and then carry on as normal, but don't pass the mixture through a sieve.

Passion fruit panna cotta

Serves three

1 leaf of gelatine

380g single cream

30g sweetener

35g sieved passion fruit pulp

Blackberry and lime panna cotta

Serves three

Blackberries are abundant in the hedges of many countries so it would be a shame not to use them in as many recipes as possible. Limes don't grow quite so well in the wilds of my neck of the woods but that's what shops are for!

330g whipping cream

70g sweetener

150g blackberries

15g lime juice (1 lime)

1½ limes zest

1 leaf of gelatine

Soak the gelatine in as much cold water as it takes to cover it for around five minutes.

Place the rest of the ingredients in a saucepan and bring to a gentle boil for 2 minutes.

Remove the pan from the heat and blitz the contents with a hand blender or in a food processor.

Pass the blackberry liquid through a fine sieve.

Squeeze any excess water from the gelatine leaf and stir into the blackberry cream.

Once the gelatine has dissolved pour the mixture into glasses.

Lightly pass the flame of a blowtorch across the surface of the panna cottas to burst any bubbles.

Chill for eight hours or overnight and serve in the glasses.

Lemon panna cotta

Serves three

Gelatine sets liquids weaker in the presence of acid, but acid sets cream more strongly than without it. Getting a harmonious balance of these competing factors is what being a Chef is all about. Or you could just follow my recipe and save a bit of time.

1 leaf of gelatine

35g sweetener

400g whipping cream

30g lemon juice (1 lemon)

Zest of ½ a lemon

Soften the gelatine in enough cold water to cover it.

Meanwhile bring the rest of the ingredients up to a brief boil in a small saucepan and remove from the heat.

Squeeze any excess water from the gelatine leaves and add them to the hot mixture.

After a minute, pass the liquid through a fine sieve to remove the lemon zest.

Pour the lemon cream into moulds and chill in a fridge for at least 6 hours.

Pumpkin pie

Serves sixteen

This started out as a pumpkin custard when I didn't have a pastry recipe that was even half decent. Like many Chefs I attempted to give this menu stalwart a modern twist, but in the end, I had to concede that sometimes it's just best not to mess around with the classics!

A 26cm baked pastry case

425g pumpkin puree

275g whipping cream

100g sweetener

5 eggs, beaten

2 tsp vanilla extract

½ tsp ginger

1 tsp cinnamon

¼ tsp nutmeg

A good pinch of ground cloves.

To lower the fat, you can replace the cream with single cream or substitute some of it with milk or even a plant-based milk.

Preheat your oven to 165°c / gas mark 3 / 325°f.

Fully combine all the ingredients in the order they are listed.

Pour the filling mix into the precooked, glazed pastry case and jiggle it gently to even it out.

Transfer the tart to the oven and bake for 35 minutes.

Remove the pie to cool for thirty minutes and then refrigerate for at least eight hours, or better overnight.

This recipe also works cooked as one large dish of pumpkin custard or in several ramekins.

Blackberry posset

Serves three

The word posset was a synonym for something simple or worthless in the way that "a trifle" is still used today. I would not recommend using it in this way nowadays though, unless you rather enjoy confusing people.

250g double cream

35g sweetener

100g blackberries

20g lime juice (from 1 lime)

Bring all the ingredients to the boil and maintain a low rolling boil for four minutes.

Blitz the liquid with a hand blender.

Pass through a fine sieve to remove any seeds.

Pour into ramekins or similar and pass the flame of a blowtorch over the surface to pop any bubbles that have formed.

Chill in the fridge for at least eight hours or overnight.

Blueberry posset

Serves three

I was told as a young chef that we eat first with our eyes. The lurid, cartoon purple of this recipe lets you know that it will taste just as vibrant as it looks. Like an oversized cartoon mallet of flavour. The presentation is up to you, but I would suggest staying away from cartoon metaphors for this.

230g double cream

50g sweetener

100g Blueberries

40g lime juice (from 2 limes)

Weigh all the ingredients into the same saucepan and blitz with a hand blender.

Bring the saucepan to a boil, swirling every now and then.

Keep at a low rolling boil for five minutes.

Pass through a fine sieve to remove the seeds.

Pour into ramekins or similar and pass the flame of a blowtorch over the surface to burst any little bubbles.

Chill in the fridge for at least eight hours or overnight.

Lemon posset

Serves four

This beautifully simple dessert has seen somewhat of a renaissance during my career. I have eaten some truly beautiful possets made with only three ingredients and this recipe keeps as true to those sweet, sour delights as I can.

500g double cream

75g sweetener

60g lemon juice (from two lemons)

Zest of 1 lemon

Simply bring all the ingredients to the boil and maintain a low rolling boil for four minutes.

Pass through your finest seive to remove the zest and pour into ramekins or similar.

Burst any bubbles on the surface with gentle use of a blowtorch.

Chill in the fridge for at least eight hours.

Passion fruit posset

Serves three

I was rather surprised to find that passion fruit might be useful as a low carb dessert component, but it really is! The strong flavour and the natural acids in the fruits lend themselves perfectly to this recipe. The only drawback here is having to sieve out the seeds from the fruit but compared to some of life's hardships I think a little light sieving is quite alright.

250g double cream

30g sweetener

30g passion fruit pulp, sieved (2 passion fruit)

A pinch of salt

Weigh all the ingredients into a saucepan and gently bring to a low rolling boil for five minutes, swirling every so often.

Pass through a fine sieve and pour into ramekins or something similar.

Gently pass the flame of a blowtorch over any bubbles to burst them.

Chill in a fridge for eight hours or overnight.

Strawberry posset

Serves three

The possets of medieval times were hot drinks of curdled cream. They were often alcoholic, spiced, served in something a bit like a teapot and eaten with a fork. None of this is commonplace now. It would be interesting to see someone eat this recipe from a teapot and use a fork though.

200g double cream

35g sweetener

100g strawberries

20g lemon juice (from 1 lemon)

Bring all the ingredients to the boil and maintain a low rolling boil for four minutes.

Blitz with a hand blender.

Pass through a fine sieve to remove any seeds.

Pour into ramekins or similar and pass the flame of a blowtorch over the surface to pop any bubbles that have formed.

Chill in the fridge for at least eight hours or overnight.

Pots de crème

Serves three

This is very similar to a crème brulée without the brulée bit. A lovely little baked custard in a pot, ramekin, cup etc. It's the kind of thing you see on menus in France with some berries or a bit of shortbread. That's the kind of simplicity that French food does so well and that doesn't always translate to menus and tastes in other countries. Even the name works best in French, because "tub of cream" just doesn't do it justice.

300g whipping cream

30g sweetener

½ a vanilla pod, seeds scraped out & reserved

2 egg yolks

1 egg

To lower the fat, you can replace the cream with single cream if you like or substitute some of it with milk or even a plant-based milk.

Bring all the ingredients except the egg up to scalding point in a saucepan and remove from the heat.

Whisk the eggs together in a bowl.

After cooling for five minutes, whisk a little of the hot cream into the egg in a slow, thin stream to "temper" them.

Preheat your oven to 140°c / gas mark 1 / 275°f.

Whisk the egg and cream mix back into the rest of the cream and return it to a gentle heat.

Whisk the custard until it thickens enough to coat the back of a wooden spoon.

Remove from the heat and pass through the finest sieve you can find.

Pour into ramekins or similar and arrange them in a deep baking tray.

Lightly pass the flame of a blowtorch over the custard to burst all the tiny bubbles on the surface.

Pour hot water around the custard pots until about halfway up.

Cover the tray with foil and pierce it a couple of times.

Carefully transfer the tray into your waiting oven. Make sure to keep it as level as possible.

Bake the lot for 30 minutes.

Remove the foil and give the tray a good tap. The custards should gently wobble a little in the middle but be rather firm on the outsides.

Carefully remove the tray from the oven and the custards from the tray. Leave to cool for ten minutes and transfer to a fridge to set for eight hours or overnight.

Variations on Pots de crème

Additions of star anise, a piece of a cinnamon quill, cardamom or allspice make very nice custard pots.

A good pinch of saffron instead of the vanilla makes a lovely dessert.

Pumpkin spice, teas and the addition of a few berries at the bottom of the ramekin are all things I have done with crème brulées and they would work very well here too.

Chocolate pots

Serves four

The name says it all here. It's a pot of chocolate. Well, not really a pot, probably a ramekin, or a cup or something. And it's not chocolate per se, it's a chocolate flavoured custard really, but chocolate flavoured custard ramekins doesn't sound quite as good. Let's just forget about the pots bit and concentrate on the chocolatey yumminess!

300g whipping cream

35g sweetener

60g butter

3 egg yolks

75g cacao, broken up

A pinch of salt

Bring all the ingredients except the egg and cacao up to a simmer in a saucepan and remove from the heat.

After a minute or so, whisk a little of the hot cream into the yolks in a slow, thin stream.

Whisk the egg and cream mix back into the rest of the liquid and return it to a gentle heat.

Whisk the custard until it thickens enough to coat the back of a wooden spoon.

Stir in the cacao until fully combined.

Pass through a fine sieve.

Pour into ramekins or something similar, like cups or glasses.

Leave to cool for ten minutes and transfer to a fridge to set for eight hours or overnight.

Variations on chocolate pots

Add aromatics like chilli or cinnamon to the cream at the beginning if you are after a South American flavour.

You could swap some or all the butter for coconut oil if you like.

To reduce the fat content, you can replace the whipping cream with single cream.

Cinnamon and coffee Pots de crème

Serves four

A friend from overseas wanted some cinnamon flavoured dessert recipes so for a few weeks I set about concentrating on that for her. This is one of my favourite recipes from that little task. I tried to emulate the Mexican flavours she loves, but I've never been to Mexico, so I don't know the Mexican coffee I was trying to recreate. It's a hard life!

450g whipping cream

50g sweetener

¼ tsp salt

5g decaffeinated instant coffee

1 cinnamon stick

¼ tsp ground cinnamon

10g 100% cacao

10g coconut oil

5 egg yolks

Bring the ingredients except the egg, cacao and coconut oil up to scalding point in a saucepan and remove from the heat.

Stir in the cacao and coconut oil until fully combined.

Whisk the eggs together in a bowl.

Whisk a little of the hot cream into the egg in a slow, thin stream.

Whisk the egg and cream mix back into the rest of the liquid and return it to a gentle heat.

Whisk the custard until it thickens enough to coat the back of a wooden spoon.

Preheat your oven to 140°c / gas mark 1 / 275°f

Remove from the heat and pass through the finest sieve you have into ramekins or similar and arrange in a deep baking tray.

Lightly pass the flame of a blowtorch over the custard before it goes in the oven to burst all the tiny bubbles.

Poor hot water around the custard pots until about halfway up.

Cover the tray with foil, pierce it a couple of times and bake the lot for 30 minutes.

Remove the foil and give the tray a good tap. The custards should gently wobble a little in the middle but be rather firm on the outsides.

Carefully remove the tray from the oven and the custards from the tray. Leave to cool for ten minutes and transfer to a fridge to set for eight hours or overnight.

Variations on Cinnamon and coffee Pots

I've read that the addition of nutmeg, orange zest and cayenne or chilli peppers are common in Mexican Café de Olla and all of these would work very well in this recipe.

To make the recipe without the cacao simply add another egg yolk to make up for the setting power of the cacao.

For a middle eastern variation just replace the cinnamon stick with some cardamom. I recommend around 10 cardamom pods for this recipe.

Chocolate roulade

Serves eight

For some reason the world is plagued by dry cake and rubbery mousses. Luckily a mousse within a cake can be light and airy, and if you fill a cake with mousse it can hardly be dry. Science!

125g ground almonds

1 tsp baking powder

1 tbsp cocoa powder

4 eggs, separated

55g sweetener

¾ tsp xanthan

200g whipping cream

30g sweetener

40g cacao

A pinch of salt

90g pasteurised egg white

Mix together all the dry sponge ingredients with the yolks and set aside.

Line a 33cm x 23cm Swiss roll tin with greaseproof paper.

Preheat your oven to 165°c / Gas mark 3 / 325°f.

Whisk the egg whites to soft peaks and gradually fold the dry ingredients through them in three batches.

Once just mixed together, spread the cake mixture across the greaseproof paper with a cranked palette knife or similar. Try to aim for a tidy rectangular shape and keep the long edges as neat as possible.

Bake for 20 minutes and remove from the oven to cool slightly.

While the sponge is baking, heat the whipping cream with the sweetener until you reach scalding point and remove from the heat.

Add the cacao, stirring occasionally until fully combined.

Whisk the egg whites and salt until soft peaks are formed and fold through the chocolate mixture in three batches until a harmonious mixture is formed.

Chill in a fridge for ten minutes.

Remove the paper-lined sponge from the swiss roll tin.

Spread the chocolate mousse across the surface of the sponge, leaving a 3cm bare gap at the edges.

With the sponge with the least neat long edge towards you, and grasping the greaseproof paper, gently fold the sponge and mousse over tightly upon itself.

Continue to roll, peeling away the paper as you go.

Gently wrap in the paper, and then in a tight layer of clingfilm.

Chill in the fridge for eight hours or overnight.

To serve, undo the clingfilm and paper covering and dust with powdered sweetener or cocoa powder.

Trim off the edges at the point where the mousse reaches and gently slice into eight portions with a hot clean knife.

Variations on a chocolate roulade

To make the dessert even more decadent, you can coat it in a layer of chocolate ganache.

100g double cream

100g butter

15g sweetener

25g cacao

Bring the ingredients except the cacao up to scalding point in a small saucepan and remove from the heat.

Break up the cacao and stir into the cream mixture.

Leave the ganache to cool slightly.

Meanwhile place the unsliced roulade in the freezer for the ten minutes.

Arrange a wire cooling rack on a deep tray.

After the ten minutes, place the roulade on the wire rack and cover with half of the ganache.

Carefully turn the roulade over and repeat with the rest of the ganache before chilling in the fridge for four hours.

Trim and slice as described above.

Hazelnut roulade

Serves eight

I remember making hazelnut roulades from a book now seventy years old when I was a young Chef. The author of that book was evacuated from Europe before the second world war because the who's who of Britain needed her cakes that much! Maybe writing this recipe might get me evacuated to a nice beach somewhere once a year.

125g ground, roasted hazelnuts

1 tsp baking powder

1 tsp cocoa powder

4 eggs, separated

55g sweetener

¾ tsp xanthan

2 leaves of gelatine

2 tbsp boiling water

20g sweetener

The seeds of a vanilla pod

300g whipping cream

Mix all the ingredients except the egg whites together.

Line a 33cm x 23cm Swiss roll tin with greaseproof paper.

Preheat your oven to 165°c / Gas mark 3 / 325°f.

Whisk the egg whites to soft peaks and gradually fold through the dry ingredients in three batches.

Once just mixed together, spread the cake mixture across the greaseproof paper. Try to aim for a tidy rectangular shape and keep the long edges as neat as possible.

Bake for 20 minutes and remove from the oven to cool slightly.

Soak the gelatine in as much cold water as it takes to cover it for around five minutes.

Whip the cream to soft peaks and set aside.

Mix the boiling water, sweetener and vanilla together.

Squeeze any excess water from the gelatine leaves and add them to the hot vanilla water.

Stir a tablespoonful of the whipped cream through the hot water mixture and then fold that back through the whipped cream.

Chill the mousse for ten minutes.

Remove the paper-lined sponge from the swiss roll tin.

Spread the vanilla mousse across the surface of the sponge, leaving a 3cm bare gap at the edges.

With the sponge with the least neat long edge towards you, and grasping the greaseproof paper, gently fold the sponge and mousse over tightly upon itself.

Continue to roll, peeling away the paper as you go.

Gently wrap in the paper, and then in a tight layer of clingfilm.

Chill in the fridge for four hours or more.

To serve, undo the clingfilm and paper covering and dust with powdered sweetener or roll in more ground hazelnuts.

Trim off the edges at the point that the mousse reaches and gently slice into eight portions with a hot clean knife.

For a quicker roulade you can simply fill the rolled sponge with whipped cream and berries and forgo the four hours chilling in favour of one hour.

Warm chocolate sponge

Serves four

I started cooking as a child by helping my mother make cakes for our afternoon teas. If you had helped then you were rewarded with the wooden spoon to lick, or the bowl if you had been particularly useful. I realised at some point that if I made the whole thing then I got to lick both the spoon and the bowl! So, motivated by a childhood greed for sweet things I learned how to make a sponge cake. This one is served hot because it is so much better that way and it gives you the excuse to cool it down a bit with some cream!

50g cacao

90g butter

60g sweetener

3 egg whites

3 egg yolks

50g ground almonds

Melt the butter, sweetener and cacao together in a Bain Marie and stir until fully combined.

Heat your oven to 165°c / gas mark 3 / 325°f.

Beat the egg whites until they will hold soft peaks.

Fold the whipped egg into the chocolate mixture in three batches.

Beat the egg yolks until pale and fold them into the mixture as well.

Carefully fold the ground almonds through the mixture.

Spoon the cake mixture into four ramekins or something similar.

Level the tops off by gently jiggling the ramekins a little.

Transfer to the oven and bake for 20 minutes.

Serve hot from the oven.

Variations on a warm chocolate sponge

You can always wait for the sponge to go cold and eat it then.

If you want a sponge that isn't bound by a ramekin, use some metal ring moulds lined with parchment and foil wrapped around their bases.

Lemon syllabub

Serves four

Syllabub is one of those medieval British desserts that we still have hanging around. Legend has it that the syllabubs of old were made by milking a cow directly onto some cider or wine, whereupon the curds and froth were eaten with a spoon and the liquid that separated was drunk through the spout of your syllabub pot. This modern recipe is much less curdled and does not require contact with any udders.

300g whipping cream

30g brandy

150g dry white wine

15g sweetener

2 whole lemons

Thinly slice off the zest of the whole lemon, trying to leave as much of the white pith behind as possible.

Blanch the zest pieces in a small saucepan of boiling water for a minute and remove them to cool down.

Empty out the lemon water and replace it with the alcohols and sweetener.

Segment the lemon that the zest came from, trying to avoid any of the bitter pith. Squeeze any juice from the remains into the saucepan.

Finely grate the zest of the other lemon into the saucepan.

Slice the zested lemon in half and strain its juice into the alcohol mixture.

Heat the contents of the saucepan until reduced by half.

If you are daring, flambéing the alcohol as it reduces will speed up the process and provide a better syllabub.

Once reduced, remove the hot liquid to cool.

Whip the cream to stiff peaks and chill.

Dice the segments of lemon.

Slice the blanched zest into very thin strips.

Fold the cream, the cooled liquid and the diced segments together and divide into glasses for serving.

Arrange the strips of zest on the tops of the syllabubs as a garnish.

Passion fruit syllabub

Serves four

Solybubbe, sallibube, sillibucke, sullibib, sillybob, sullybub, sullibub, sullabub, sellibub, sillebube, sillibub, syllabub.

200g dry white wine

30g gin

20g sweetener

90g passion fruit pulp, sieved

300g whipping cream

1 passion fruit

Add the alcohols and sweetener to a small saucepan and heat until reduced by half.

If you like, flambéing the alcohol as it reduces will speed up the process and provide a better syllabub.

Once reduced, remove from the heat and stir in the passion fruit pulp.

Whip the cream to stiff peaks and chill.

Fold the fruity alcohol mixture into the cream until almost fully combined and divide into glasses for serving.

Chill for at least 1 hour.

Scrape out the seeds and pulp from the remaining passionfruit to decorate the tops of the syllabubs before serving.

If you feel that you need the fibre, you can leave the seeds in the passion fruit pulp, they are perfectly edible and provide a nice little crunch every now and then.

Raspberry syllabub

Serves four

Like the English desserts trifle and posset, the syllabub is used as a synonym for something derogatory. In this case something "insubstantial". I wonder if the same could be true of European desserts. For example, Tiramisu could be another word for having a soaked bottom, as in "it were so bloomin' wet on me bike I were proper tiramisu!"

Or not.

80g raspberries

20g sweetener

45g dry white wine

15g kirsch

¼ tsp rosewater

300g whipping cream

120g raspberries

Bring the first lot of ingredients up to a simmer for a minute and remove from the heat.

Pass the mixture through a fine sieve and leave to cool.

Whip the cream to stiff peaks.

Fold the whole raspberries and the raspberry purée through the cream.

Transfer to serving glasses and chill in a fridge until served.

Summer syllabub

Serves four

I love the name "syllabub", it's just so weird. There are umpteen other variations for the name from ages past, but my favourite must be "solybubbe", which I am told should be pronounced like "soily boob"!

200g dry white wine

30g kirsch or brandy

15g sweetener

100g strawberries

100g raspberries

300g whipping cream

Ground sweetener

Add the alcohols, sweetener and half of each of the fruits to a small saucepan and heat until the liquid has reduced by half.

If you like, flambéing the alcohol as it reduces will speed up the process and provide a better syllabub.

Once reduced, remove from the heat.

Press the fruit and alcohol through a fine sieve to remove any seeds.

Roughly dice the remaining strawberries and add them to the liquid.

Whip the cream to stiff peaks and chill.

Fold three quarters of the fruity alcohol mixture into the cream until almost fully combined and divide into four glasses for serving.

Chill for at least 1 hour.

Garnish with the remaining berry liquid, topped with the raspberries and a dusting of ground sweetener.

Other berries will work here but I suggest you include raspberries as half the fruit.

If you prefer to leave the berries' seeds in the syllabub, you will need to blitz the mixture instead of passing it through a sieve.

Bakewell tart

Serves sixteen

Bakewell tart is just about the perfect dessert for a carb reducing makeover. Being mostly almonds, the adaptation is straightforward, except for making a ketogenic jam! Which is why I have made a fluid gel-jam instead. Don't worry, once you make the gel you will realise that it's just got a silly name and is also pretty simple.

For the raspberry fluid jam...

160g raspberries

2 tsp agar agar

2 tsp sweetener

2 tbsp water

A pinch of salt

75g raspberries

Cider vinegar to taste

Put the Agar, the sweetener and the water into a small saucepan with the 160g of raspberries on top.

After a few minutes of gentle heating, blitz the raspberry mixture with a hand blender and return to the heat.

Bring the mix up to a boil and keep it there for three minutes, then set aside to cool.

Chill overnight in a fridge.

Blitz the raspberry gel with a hand blender and correct the acidity with the cider vinegar, it should be sweet but a little sharp too.

Mash the remaining raspberries with a fork and stir into the fluid gel.

Store covered, in the fridge.

For the tart...

A 26cm baked pastry case in the tart ring

Raspberry fluid jam

250g ground almonds

250g butter, soft

125g sweetener

5 eggs

2 tsp baking powder

50g double cream

35g flaked almonds

Set your oven to 165°g / gas mark 3 / 325°f.

Cream together your butter and sweetener until noticeably paler.

Add the other ingredients except either lot of almonds and mix thoroughly.

Add the ground almonds and beat to incorporate a little air.

Spread some of your raspberry fluid gel-jam across the cooked pastry case. Try to avoid missing any spots.

Carefully spread the almond mixture across the pastry case trying not to disturb the raspberry jam too much.

Level the mixture and sprinkle over the flaked almonds. Give the almonds a gentle press into the batter and transfer to the oven for 40 minutes.

Reduce the heat to 140°c / gas mark 1 / 275°f for a further 20 minutes.

Remove the tart to cool down and then move it to a fridge to chill overnight.

Once chilled, remove the tart from its ring and slice with a sharp knife then gently reheat or eat cold.

Blueberry tart

Serves sixteen

This recipe will work with blueberries, brylocks, whortleberries, dyeberries, windberries, bleaberries, wimberries, whorts, bilberries, trackleberries, whinberries, hartberries, wineberries, hurts, brimbelles, myrtle berries, hurtleberries, huckleberries, fraughans, worts, and even myrtilles.

A 26cm baked pastry case in the tart ring

120 almond butter

50g butter

60g sweetener

200g ground almonds

2 eggs

2 yolks

180g single cream

Zest of a lemon, finely grated

800g blueberries

Add all the ingredients for the filling, except the blueberries, to a large bowl one by one, beating well with each addition.

Meanwhile preheat your oven to 177°c / gas mark 4 / 350°f.

Fold half of the blueberries through the filling mixture.

Evenly transfer the filling to the pastry case and gently smooth the top a little.

Poke the remaining blueberries into the batter so that some of each berry is not submerged in the mixture.

Bake for 40 minutes and remove from the oven to cool for an hour or so.

Chill in the fridge for eight hours or preferably overnight.

Once chilled, remove the tart from its ring and slice with a clean, sharp knife.

Chocolate ganache tart

Serves sixteen

For years the excuse to yell tart at someone who is preparing, handling or serving one of these things has brought a smile to many a face in kitchens across the world. Shout pie at someone and you might get a very different look in return!

A 26cm baked pastry case in the tart ring

500 double cream

500g butter

75g sweetener

125g cacao, broken up

Bring the cream, butter and sweetener up to boiling point in a saucepan and remove from the heat.

Stir in the cacao.

Once fully combined, pour the mixture into the pastry case.

Gently pass the flame of a blowtorch over the surface of the ganache to burst any bubbles.

Refrigerate for at least eight hours or overnight.

Once chilled, remove the tart from its ring and slice with a clean, sharp knife.

Crunchy peanut butter tart

Serves sixteen

I never really liked the way that peanut butter sticks to the roof of your mouth. This can be overcome by means of dilution: with chocolate spread, with cream, or in this case with the rest of a tart!

A 26cm baked pastry case in the tart ring

200g double cream

180g butter

25g sweetener

A pinch of salt

60g cacao, broken up

250g ground almonds

110g sweetener

5 eggs

300g single cream

400g crunchy peanut butter

Scald the cream, butter and sweetener with the salt and remove from the heat.

Stir in the cacao every couple of minutes until it has all melted in and become smooth.

Poor the ganache onto the pastry case and chill for at least fifteen minutes before moving on to making the rest of the tart.

Heat your oven to 177°c / gas mark 4 / 350°f.

Add the ingredients for the filling to a mixer and beat well until well combined.

Spoon the mixture into the pastry case, gently smooth the top a little and bake for 35minutes.

Remove from the oven to cool and chill for eight hours or overnight.

Once chilled, remove the tart from its ring and slice with a clean, hot knife.

Variations on a crunchy peanut butter tart

This recipe will work well with other nut or seed butters or smooth peanut butter.

Baked custard tart

Serves sixteen

This is the first recipe I did for this book, so it occupies a special place in my heart. Well, it's the first recipe I got right really.

A 26cm baked pastry case in its tart ring

3 eggs

5 egg yolks

750g whipping cream

90g sweetener

Fresh nutmeg

To reduce the fat a little you can use single cream or replace some cream with milk.

Scald the cream with the sweetener and remove from the heat.

Preheat your oven to 140°c / gas mark 1 / 275°f.

While the cream is cooling you can whisk the eggs with the yolks to make a smooth mixture.

Pour some of the hot cream into the egg mixture while you whisk. Then whisk this mix back into the rest of the cream.

Return the custard mixture to the heat and whisk continuously until it has thickened enough to cover the back of a wooden spoon. Use a Bain Marie instead if you are worried about overcooking.

Pour the hot custard through a fine sieve, pour into the prepared pastry case and gently transfer it to your oven.

Pass the flame of a blowtorch over the custard to burst all the tiny bubbles.

Bake for 30 minutes.

It should have a gentle wobble in the middle when you tap it but otherwise be immobile.

Remove the tart to somewhere it can chill at room temperature and grate over your nutmeg while still warm.

Chill at least eight hours in the fridge or overnight.

Once chilled, remove the tart from its ring.

To cut the tart a clean, hot knife would be best.

Variations on a custard tart

Manchester tart

Serves sixteen

Add a teaspoon of vanilla extract to the cream before it has the egg added.

Spread one 225g quantity of raspberry "fluid jam" on the base before gently covering with the custard. A ladle etc. would be a good idea here.

Swap the nutmeg for 25g of desiccated coconut. Sprinkle the coconut evenly over the custard before transferring it into the oven to bake.

Gianduja cremeaux tart

Serves sixteen

Gianduja is a funky name for hazelnut chocolate, and cremeaux just means creamy. So basically, it means creamy hazelnut chocolate tart. Another option would have been to call it a "tarte gianduja au crème collée", which literally means a hazelnut chocolate glued cream tart, which is just silly.

A 26cm baked pastry case in its tart ring

600g single cream

85g sweetener

5 egg yolks

100g cacao

150g hazelnut butter

A pinch of salt

3 leaves of gelatine

Soak the gelatine leaves in as much cold water as it takes to cover them for around five minutes.

Bring the cream and sweetener up to scalding point in a saucepan big enough to include the other ingredients too.

Remove from the heat.

After a minute or so, whisk a little of the hot cream into the egg yolks and then whisk them back into the rest of the cream.

Return the saucepan to the heat and continue to whisk until the custard is thick enough to coat the back of a wooden spoon.

Remove from the heat.

Stir in the cacao until a harmonious mixture is formed.

Squeeze any excess water from the leaves of gelatine and add them to the chocolate custard.

Add the hazelnut butter and salt to the custard and stir until uniformly combined.

Strain the mixture through a fine sieve and pour into the pastry case.

Briefly pass the flame of a blowtorch over the surface of the tart to burst any bubbles.

Chill for at least eight hours or overnight.

Once chilled, remove the tart from its ring and carefully slice with a clean hot knife.

Gooseberry tart

Serves sixteen

Around my neck off the woods a lot of people call these hairy little berries goosegogs, I have no idea why. I do know that they are very much worth battling the thorns of the gooseberry bush for, or of course a brief haggle with a greengrocer.

A 26cm baked pastry case in its tart ring

200g ground almonds

200g butter

110g sweetener

4 egg yolks

3 eggs

¾ tsp baking powder

⅛ tsp xanthan

20g water

125g trimmed gooseberries

30g flaked almonds

Preheat your oven to 165°c / gas mark 3 / 325°f.

Beat together the butter and sweetener until the mixture goes pale.

Add the eggs and beat again until combined.

Add the ground almonds, the water and the powders and give the whole lot a good mixing until it looks uniform.

Transfer this batter to the pastry case and smooth the top off with a palette knife.

Poke the gooseberries into the batter in the tart case in evenly spaced intervals.

Poke the flaked almonds into the spaces between the gooseberries.

Transfer the tart to the oven and cook for 40 minutes.

Remove from the oven to cool and chill for eight hours or overnight.

Remove from the tart ring and slice with a clean sharp knife.

Lemon tart

Serves twelve

For years I played with different lemon tart recipes trying to find one I was satisfied with, eventually concentrating on several iterations of lemon curd tarts, but they were all based on other people's ideas. This one is mine and I'm super proud of it. It won't get me a Nobel Prize or save a life, but it does taste great and it's not just another version of a version.

A 26cm baked pastry case in its tart ring

500g double cream

220g lemon juice

160g sweetener

The grated zest of six lemons

A pinch of salt

9 eggs

4 egg yolks

Preheat your oven to 140°c / gas mark 1 / 275°f.

Bring the cream, lemon, salt and Truvia to a boil and simmer gently for a minute.

Remove the hot cream mixture from the heat and leave to cool a little.

After cooling for a minute, whisk some of the creamy liquid into the eggs and then whisk that mixture back into the rest of the creamy stuff.

Strain through a seive to remove the lemon zest.

Pour the lemon custard into the tart case.

Gently pass the flame of a blowtorch over the surface of the lemon tart to burst all the small bubbles on the top.

Carefully transfer into your oven.

Bake for 40 minutes.

The tart should gently jiggle when tapped on the side.

Remove from the oven to cool for 30 minutes and transfer to the fridge to set for at least eight hours or overnight.

Once chilled, remove the tart from its ring and slice with a clean, sharp, hot knife.

Passion fruit tart

Serves sixteen

Passing the passion fruit pulp is an annoying process. Getting all the flavourful pulp away from those pesky seeds takes some time and a bit of effort. Imagine if we had never invented the sieve though! What a grim world that would be, without the smoothness and refinement that it makes possible. It would hardly be worth living!

A 26cm baked pastry case in its tart ring

600g single cream

10 passion fruit pulped; seeds removed

30g lemon juice (1 lemon)

¼ tsp agar agar flakes

25g sweetener

5 egg yolks

Bring all the ingredients except the egg yolks up to a simmer for 3 minutes in a saucepan and remove from the heat.

After a minute of cooling, whisk a little of the hot cream mixture into the egg yolks, and then add that back to the rest of the hot liquid.

Return the saucepan to the heat and whisk on a low heat until the egg yolks cause the custard to thicken enough to coat the back of a wooden spoon.

Pass the mixture through a fine sieve and pour into the pastry case.

Gently pass the flame of a blowtorch across the surface of the tart to burst any bubbles.

Chill for at least eight hours or overnight.

Once chilled, remove the tart from its ring and slice with a clean, sharp knife.

Peanut butter tart

Serves sixteen

I suppose everyone knows that a peanut isn't a nut but rather a legume. Being a bit of a culinary geek, I was always rather pleased with myself when a question that referred to this fact came up in a pub quiz. Thanks to the internet, my usefulness in these affairs has become more and more tenuous and my knowledge need fully more obscure. Luckily, I don't tend to take part in such contests anymore because I'm digging into delicious tarts.

A 26cm baked pastry case in its tart ring

650g smooth peanut butter

350g single cream

200g soured cream

120g sweetener

4 eggs

A pinch of salt

Add the ingredients for the filling to a mixer and beat well after each addition.

Heat your oven to 140°c / gas mark 1 / 275°f.

When all the parts are combined into a smooth harmonious mixture, pour it into the pastry case.

Lightly pass the flame of a blowtorch across the surface of the tart to burst any bubbles.

Bake for 40 minutes.

Remove from the oven to cool for an hour.

Chill in a fridge for eight hours or overnight.

Remove from the ring mould and slice with a hot, clean knife.

Variations on a peanut butter tart

This recipe works well with almond, cashew, macadamia and other nut butters if you don't want to use peanut butter.

Peanut butter and chocolate tart

Serves sixteen

I know I pair peanut and chocolate quite a bit. In the winter months when fruit isn't in season, I don't have many options for recipes to develop. There is passion fruit, citrus, chocolate and nuts, and it happens to be the time of year that my regular job is quietest, so it's when I get the most done. Also, I really like the salty sweet combination, and it does happen to taste rather good.

A 26cm baked pastry case in its tart ring

200g double cream

180g butter

30g sweetener

65g cacao, broken up

5 eggs

400g peanut butter, smooth

105g sweetener

250g ground almonds

300g single cream

A pinch of salt

To make the ganache, bring all the ingredients except the cacao up to a simmer and remove from the heat.

Stir in the cacao until fully combined.

Preheat your oven to 175°c / gas mark 4 / 350°f.

Pour the ganache into the pastry case and chill in a fridge.

Beat the ingredients for the peanut custard together one by one starting with the eggs.

Pour the peanut mixture onto the chilled ganache and level with a cranked palette knife.

Bake for 35 minutes.

Remove to cool for thirty minutes.

Chill for eight hours or preferably overnight.

Once chilled, remove the tart from its ring and slice with a clean, sharp knife.

Peanut butter ganache tart

Serves sixteen

I never really ate peanut butter on toast or bread, but when I discovered how well it went with chocolate flavours I was hooked. For desserts, a nice punchy flavour like this is brilliant. This is a flavour combination that I will keep going back to and that I will keep having seconds of.

A 26cm baked pastry case in its tart ring

525g double cream

75g sweetener

75g cacao, broken up

450g smooth peanut butter

120g cream cheese

A pinch of salt

To reduce the fat, you can swap the double cream for whipping cream and the cream cheese could be a fat free variety.

Scald the cream with the sweetener and remove from the heat.

Once off the heat add the cacao to the cream mix and stir until combined.

Add the peanut butter to the cream mixture and stir again until combined.

Now add the cream cheese and stir again until you have a nice even mixture.

Pour the ganache into the centre of your tart case and refrigerate for at least eight hours or overnight.

Once chilled, remove the tart from its ring and slice with a clean, sharp and hot knife.

Variations on a peanut butter tart

This recipe works well with almond, cashew, macadamia and other nut butters if you don't want to use peanut.

Rhubarb panna cotta tart

Serves sixteen

Rhubarb isn't just for school dinner crumbles, but it must have gained a bad name from a million poorly made ones that probably got their contents from tins. I first experienced tinned rhubarb a few years ago and I really think the only use for that brown sludge is in horror films. The fresh stuff is a very different matter and I like it so much that half of my kitchen garden is dedicated to growing it.

A 26cm baked pastry case in its tart ring

1000g single cream

140g sweetener

3 leaves of gelatine

5 egg yolks

350g rhubarb

¼ tsp rosewater

Weigh out the rhubarb without any of the leaves, they are a little poisonous!

Chop the stalks and put them, with the rosewater, in a microwave safe bowl and cover with a lid or clingfilm.

Microwave the rhubarb pieces for ten minutes or as long as it takes to reduce them to a pulp.

Meanwhile soak the gelatine leaves in as much cold water as it takes to cover them for about five minutes.

Scald the cream with the sweetener and salt and remove from the heat.

After a minute, whisk a little of the hot cream through the egg yolks and then whisk them back through the cream.

Return the cream mixture to a gentle heat and whisk until thickened then remove from the heat.

Squeeze out any excess water from the gelatine leaves and add them with the rhubarb, to the hot custard and stir to dissolve.

Blitz the rhubarb custard with a hand blender or through a food processor and pass through a fine sieve.

Place the pastry case in the fridge and carefully pour the liquid into the tart case.

Briefly pass a lit blowtorch over the surface of the liquid to burst any bubbles.

Chill for eight hours or overnight.

Once chilled, remove the tart from its ring and slice with a clean, sharp knife.

Variations on a panna cotta tart

Two tone rhubarb

Peel off the colourful outer layer of the raw rhubarb and microwave that separately from the rest.

Separate 200g of the hot custard after it thickens.

Add the deeper coloured rhubarb to the 200g of custard and chill in the fridge.

Continue with the rest of the tart normally.

After the tart has had four hours to chill remove the separate rhubarb and custard from the fridge.

Gently warm the custard until it returns to a liquid.

Blitz and pass the warm custard and pour onto the top of the chilling tart.

Briefly pass a lit blowtorch over the surface again and let the tart finish setting.

Blackberry

Replace the rhubarb and rosewater with 250g of blackberries and 1 tsp of lemon juice and reduce the sweetener to 100g.

Otherwise proceed normally with the recipe.

Blueberry and lime

Replace the rhubarb with 250g of blueberries.

Swap the rosewater for the juice and finely grated zest of a lime.

Reduce the sweetener to 120g.

Otherwise proceed normally with the recipe.

Raspberry

Replace the rhubarb and rosewater with 250g of raspberries and 2 tsp of lemon juice and reduce the sweetener to 120g.

Otherwise proceed normally with the recipe.

Walnut tart

Serves twelve

I have heard several different definitions of what makes a tart a tart and a torte a torte. Honestly, I'm still not sure where the line between them is, but this one is most definitely a torte. Maybe.

A 26cm baked pastry case in its tart ring

250g butter, soft

140g sweetener

4 egg yolks

4 eggs

250g walnuts, ground

1 tsp baking powder

35g single cream

100g walnuts, crushed

20g cacao, finely grated

¼ tsp xanthan

Preheat your oven to 165°c / gas mark 3 / 325°f.

Add the ingredients for the torte to a mixing bowl one at a time starting at the top of the list.

Beat well with each addition.

Place the pastry case on a suitable metal tray and slowly transfer the torte mixture into it.

Bake the torte for 35 minutes.

Remove from the oven to cool down for thirty minutes.

Chill in the fridge for eight hours or more.

Once chilled, remove the tart from its ring and slice with a clean, sharp knife.

Tarte au chocolat

Serves sixteen

I had to include a recipe for a classic chocolate tart in this book, so I set about making one as traditionally as I could. I didn't finish off very traditionally when I decided to use yoghurt, but that hint of sourness really elevates the tart. Honestly, there isn't a great deal that is very traditional about the recipe, but you wouldn't know to look at the end result, which is rather the point.

A 26cm baked pastry case in its tart ring

750g double cream

85g sweetener

A pinch of salt

100g natural yoghurt

2 egg yolks

5 eggs

150g cacao, broken up

Heat your oven to 140°c / gas mark 1 / 275°f.

Bring the cream, sweetener and salt up to boiling point in a saucepan and remove from the heat.

Whisk the yoghurt into the cream mixture.

Whisk the yolks and whole eggs together.

Take a little of the warm dairy mixture and whisk it into the eggs, then whisk that back into the rest of the dairy.

Return the saucepan to a gentle heat and whisk continuously until the custard becomes thick enough to coat the back of a wooden spoon.

Add the cacao to the hot custard and stir until a smooth homogenous mixture is formed.

Pass the chocolate mixture through a fine sieve and pour into the pastry case.

Lightly pass the flame of a blowtorch across the surface of the chocolate tart to burst any small bubbles.

Transfer the tart to the oven and cook for 30 minutes.

Remove somewhere to cool for 30 minutes before chilling in the fridge for at least eight hours or overnight.

Once chilled, remove the tart from its ring and slice with a clean, warm knife.

ies
cao

ZUELAN BLACK

ARENERO CACAO

CACAO · NUT & SPICE

Brown butter chocolate torte

Serves sixteen

I think it's fair to say that most people like chocolate, some people really like it. I really like brown butter. So, when there is a chance to combine brown butter and chocolate I always do. That way I get to lick the spoon afterwards. And the bowl. And then eat the trimmings. And a slice. Or maybe two.

240g butter

200g cacao, broken up

200g sweetener

240g ground almonds

6 eggs, separated

A pinch of salt

Weigh out the butter into a small saucepan and gently heat until melted and foaming.

Once foamy swirl the pan a little to check the colour of the milk solids that by now should have collected at the bottom.

Keep checking the milk solids in this way every ten seconds or so.

Around the same time that the foaming subsides a little you should notice a nutty smell and upon swirling the butter you will notice that the milk solids have begun to brown.

Remove the saucepan from the heat and continue to gently swirl the pan for around a minute.

Add the sweetener to the slightly cooled brown butter.

Add the cacao the butter, stirring a few times until a homogenous mixture is formed.

Heat your oven to 165°c / gas mark 3 / 325°f.

Whisk the egg whites to soft peaks.

Whisk the egg yolks into the brown butter ganache.

Gently fold the egg whites into the chocolate mix in three batches.

Transfer the batter into a lined 20cm springform tin, cake tin or silicone mould and bake for 30 minutes.

Remove from the oven to cool and chill for at least four hours before unmoulding and serving.

Chocolate hazelnut torte

Serves twelve

This started out as a cherry and chocolate frangipane tart. As you can probably tell, it went through quite a few revisions to get where it is now. It wasn't just an excuse to eat all those different attempts. Probably.

100g hazelnut butter

75g walnut oil

110g sweetener

3 egg yolks

3 eggs

140g hazelnuts, ground

30g cocoa powder

A pinch of salt

⅛ tsp xanthan

¾ tsp baking powder

1 tbsp water

1 tbsp brandy

30g hazelnuts, crushed

25g cocoa nibs

Preheat your oven to 165°c / gas mark 3 / 325°f.

Add the ingredients for the torte to a mixing bowl one at a time starting at the top of the list.

Beat well with each addition.

Place a greased 24cm springform tin on a suitable metal tray and slowly transfer the torte mixture into it.

Bake the mix for 40 minutes.

Remove from the oven to cool down for thirty minutes.

Chill in the fridge for four hours or more.

For the ganache...

20g hazelnuts, crushed

75g double cream

75g butter

15g sweetener

25g cacao, broken up

To make the ganache, scald the first four ingredients in a small saucepan and remove from the heat.

Stir the cacao into the nutty mixture.

Remove the torte from the mould and freeze it for around five minutes.

Remove from the freezer and place on a wire cooling rack above a deep tray.

Give the ganache a good stir and gently pour it over the torte so it drips down the sides a little.

Chill in the fridge for four or more hours.

Remove from the wire rack before portioning with a hot clean knife.

DARK CH
ABSO
BLA
100% COCOA.

innovative british cho

Chocolate & Peanut torte

Serves twelve

After developing about a hundred recipes for these books I realised that everything had dairy in it, so I had a go at going dairy free as well as sugar free. It turns out that replacing dairy doesn't have to mean a loss of flavour or losing that desire to eat the entire recipe in one sitting. Which is nice.

150g coconut milk, from a tin

100g sweetener

A pinch of salt

4 egg yolks

200g peanut butter

75g cacao, finely grated

7 egg whites (210g)

Bring the coconut milk, sweetener and salt up to a brief boil and remove from the heat.

After a minute, take a little of the hot liquid and whisk it into the egg yolks.

Whisk the tempered egg yolk back into the rest of the coconut milk mixture and return to a gentle heat.

Whisk continuously until thick enough to coat the back of a wooden spoon and remove from the heat.

Stir in the peanut butter until fully combined.

Stir in the cacao.

Heat your oven to 175°c / gas mark 4 / 350°f.

Beat the egg whites to soft peaks.

Fold the egg whites through the peanut mixture in three batches.

Gently transfer the mixture to a 25cm springform tin or silicone.

Bake for 45 minutes.

Chill fully for at least eight hours before unmoulding.

Gianduja torte

Serves twelve

Gianduja is a marvellous word, clearly too flamboyant to be English, but perhaps not so easily recognisable as Italian until you try pronouncing it with a stereotypical Italian accent!

Go on, you know you want to.

180g double cream

180g sweetener

120g cacao, broken up

300g hazelnut butter

60g hazelnuts, ground

6 egg whites

A pinch of salt

4 egg yolks

Bring the cream and sweetener up to boiling point and remove from the heat.

Drop the cacao into the hot liquid and stir occasionally until combined.

Stir in the hazelnut butter and ground hazelnuts until a smooth mixture is achieved.

Beat the egg whites and salt together until they will hold soft peaks.

Fold the whipped egg into the nutty mixture in three batches.

Beat the egg yolks until pale and fold them into the mixture as well.

Heat your oven to 165°c / gas mark 3 / 325°f.

Gently transfer your torte mixture into a 24cm springform cake tin and chill in your fridge for 20 minutes.

Bake the torte for 30 minutes.

Remove from the oven to cool for another 30 minutes before chilling in a fridge overnight.

Tiramisu

Serves eight

Tiramisu means pick me up but I'm not sure whether that is because of the coffee or the booze. When I worked in an Italian restaurant, I used to put an awful lot of booze in there. I used brandy, marsala and amaretto, but we don't want that much sugar in there. I also used espresso, freshly made by the bar staff, which you can use too, but in case you don't have a bar, a barman and an espresso machine I have written the recipe with stuff from a jar.

For the sponge....

30g butter, soft

65g sweetener

1 egg

3 egg yolks

1 tsp baking powder

⅛ tsp xanthan

150g ground almonds

3 egg whites

Heat your oven to 165°c / gas mark 3 / 325°f.

Mix all the ingredients except the egg whites together one by one starting at the top of the list, and beat well with each addition.

Whisk the egg whites until they form soft peaks and fold them into the rest of the recipe a third at a time.

Once smoothly combined, spread the mixture onto a tray lined with greaseproof paper, to a 2cm thickness.

Bake for 20 minutes and remove from the oven to cool.

For the coffee.....

3 tsp instant coffee

100g hot, boiled water

10g sweetener

35g brandy

50g dry sherry

While the sponge cake cools, prepare the coffee by pouring the just boiled water onto the instant coffee.

Add the sweetener and stir to dissolve.

Add the alcohols and stir again.

Once the sponge cake is fully cooled, cut fingers, rounds, squares etc. from it.

Briefly dip half of each of them one by one in the warm coffee mixture.

Cover the base of your tray or serving dish with the slices of sponge so that the dipped half of the slice faces upwards.

For the mascarpone....

4 eggs, separated

1kg mascarpone

50g sweetener

Cacao or cocoa powder for dusting

Beat together the egg yolks, the sweetener and the mascarpone until smooth and fully combined.

Whisk the egg whites to stiff peaks and gently fold together with the mascarpone mixture.

Spread a layer of the cheese mixture on the sponge.

Repeat the sponge and cheese layers, ending with a mascarpone layer on top.

Lightly dust the top with cocoa powder or grated cacao.

Chill in a fridge for at least 4 hours.

Heat your oven to 165°c / gas mark 3 / 325°f.

Mix all the ingredients except the egg whites together.

Whisk the egg whites until they form soft peaks and fold them into the rest of the recipe a third at a time.

Once just amalgamated, spread the mixture onto a tray lined with greaseproof paper, to a depth of around 1cm.

Bake for 20 minutes and remove from the oven to cool.

Once cool to the touch, peel away the paper and trim off the edges of the sponge.

Cut into fingers, square, rounds etc. according to the size and shape of the glass or bowl that the trifle is being served in, and place the sponge at the bottom of it.

For the fruit jelly....

2 sheets of gelatine

250g boiling water

250g frozen berries

30g sweetener

Soak the gelatine until soft in enough cold water to cover it.

Combine the boiling water, the sweetener and the berries.

Once soft, squeeze any excess water from the gelatine leaves and add them to the hot berry liquid.

Once the gelatine is fully dissolved, spoon the berry liquid over the sponge cake in the glasses etc. Try to distribute the berries and liquid evenly.

Place the glasses etc. in a fridge to chill for at least an hour before moving on to the custard.

For the custard....

9 egg yolks

450g whipping cream

40g sweetener

The seeds from one vanilla pod

Scald the cream with the vanilla, salt and sweetener, and remove from the heat to cool.

After a minute, whisk a little of the cream mixture into the egg yolks and then whisk the egg mix back into the hot cream.

Cook the custard in a Bain Marie until thick enough to coat the back of a wooden spoon and remove from the heat to cool.

When the custard is around body temperature, pass it through a fine sieve or chinois and devide it among the trifle glasses.

Chill in a fridge for at least four hours before finishing with whipped cream.

For the whipped cream....

150g whipping cream

5g sweetener

Whip the cream and sweetener together until they form stiff peaks, and pipe equally onto the trifles.

Variations on a trifle

For a sherry trifle...

Simply wet the sponge with a little dry sherry before moving on to the fruit jelly part of the recipe.

This works well with brandy or kirsch too.

For a tipsy laird...

Wet the sponge with a little good Scotch whisky.

Forgo the fruit jelly entirely in favour of lots of fresh raspberries.

Sprinkle a few toasted flaked almonds over the top of the whipped cream when assembled.

For a trifle with a vegetarian agar agar jelly....

4g agar agar flakes

250g boiling water

250g frozen berries

30g Truvia

Combine the boiling water, agar agar, the sweetener and the berries in a small saucepan.

Bring the saucepan's contents to a boil and simmer for 3 minutes.

Remove from the heat to cool for a few minutes

Spoon the berry liquid over the sponge cake in the glasses etc. Try to distribute the berries and liquid evenly.

Place the glasses etc. in a fridge to chill for at least an hour before moving on to the custard.

Walnut whip

Serves three

Since the classical era there was a system called the doctrine of signatures. This taught that a plant which shared characteristics with a part of the body would treat problems stemming from that body part. Walnut halves look a lot like brains, and I am told, the human prostate, so they were thought to be good for brain and prostate health, and in this case those old Greeks were spot on. Which is rather weird.

100g walnuts

20g walnut oil

15g cacao, broken up

15g sweetener

50g crème fraiche

100g whipping cream

Microwave the walnuts on full power for 2 minutes and transfer them to a food processor.

Blitz the hot nuts until they start to turn into walnut butter.

Add the walnut oil and continue to blitz until well liquified.

Pass through a fine sieve onto the cacao.

After a minute, stir the mixture until the cacao is fully combined.

Stir in the sweetener.

Stir in the crème fraiche.

Whip the cream to soft peaks.

Mix a little of the whipped cream through the walnut paste.

Fold the walnut paste through the whipped cream and divide amongst serving glasses, ramekins, bowls etc.

Chill in a fridge for at least eight hours.

Variations on walnut whip

Obviously, you can replace the nuts here with other nuts. I would only recommend hazelnuts and pecans.

Replacing the walnut oil with truffle oil makes a lovely change.

Chocolate ice cream

I know it is silly, but I went off chocolate for years. I had eaten my way through so much chocolate at work that the lower quality stuff in shops and even the kinds I cooked with had lost their appeal. It took a long time and some very high-quality cacao to get me back on the horse (the chocolate horse). People talk about the innocence of childhood, and while they probably aren't referring to a lack of knowledge of cacao, they really should be.

350g double cream

200g water

55g sweetener

½ tsp xanthan

60g vegetable glycerine

¼ tsp salt

3 egg yolks

45g cacao

25g cacao nibs

Place the first six ingredients in a saucepan, bring to just under the boil, and remove from the heat.

After a minute whisk some of the warm mix into the yolks and then whisk that back into the whole.

Return to a low heat and whisk continuously until thickened enough to coat the back of a wooden spoon.

Remove from the heat and add the cacao, stirring occasionally until combined.

Pass through a fine sieve and refrigerate for eight hours or preferably overnight.

Churn the mix in an ice cream machine according to the manufacturer's instructions and add the cacao nibs in the last ten minutes, or simply omit them for a smoother dessert.

Freeze for at least eight hours.

Variations on chocolate ice cream

Swap the cacao nibs for some toasted hazelnuts or simply add them with the nibs.

Add cinnamon, chilli powder or cardamom if you like. They all work well with cacao or chocolate.

Strawberry cheesecake ice cream

As a child you would always be given strawberry, vanilla and chocolate ice creams together, as if they complimented each other. The other two invariably tasted fine but the strawberry one was always more than a little artificial tasting and just pink. I have not tried to redress the balance or anything, I just made this recipe up one night and it turned out particularly well.

300g cream cheese

300g strawberries, hulled

50g double cream

40g sweetener

½ tsp xanthan

70g vegetable glycerine

3 egg yolks

Place all the ingredients except the yolks in a small saucepan and blitz the lot with a hand blender.

Bring the mixture just up to the point of boiling and remove from the heat with the occasional stir.

After a minute whisk some of the warm mix into the yolks and then whisk that back into the whole.

Return to a low heat and whisk continuously until thickened enough to coat the back of a spoon.

Remove from the heat and blitz with the hand blander again.

Pass through a fine sieve and refrigerate for eight hours or preferably overnight.

Churn the mix in an ice cream machine according to the manufacturer's instructions.

Freeze for eight hours or overnight.

Vanilla ice cream

Ice cream has always been my comfort food, you might even go as far as to say that I'm an ice cream addict or even that I have an ice cream problem. I do. I have several ice cream problems; it takes so long to make, there's never enough of it, it goes so quickly and everybody else is always eating mine!

400g double cream

200g water

55g sweetener

70g vegetable glycerine

1 tsp vanilla extract

1 vanilla pod, split and seeds scraped

A pinch of salt

½ tsp xanthan

3 egg yolks

Put all the ingredients except the yolks in a small saucepan and gently bring up to boiling point, whisking occasionally.

Remove from the heat and allow to cool for a minute.

Whisk a little of the warm liquid into the yolks in a thin stream to cook them a little.

Whisk the egg back into the cream etc. in the pan and give it all a good stir.

Return the pan to a very low heat and continue to whisk around the sides and base until the mixture has thickened enough to coat the back of a wooden spoon.

Leave to cool for ten minutes.

Chill in your fridge overnight.

Strain the mixture into your ice cream maker's bowl and churn according to the instructions. Mine takes just under an hour.

Freeze for at least eight hours to harden up, or you can just eat it straight out of the machine if you really want.

You may want to reduce the fat content a little, but this will increase the hardness. Replacing 100g of cream with water or milk is as far as I would suggest going.

Agar agar pastry

I saw someone using gelatine as a gluten replacement and wondered if the same could be done with agar agar for a vegetarian pastry. This pastry recipe might have actually turned out to be my best one for most applications and all thanks to those vegetarians and the crazy person who decided that gelatinous pastry sounded good.

2 tsp agar agar flakes

50g sweetener

A pinch of salt

2 eggs

25g coconut oil

25g butter, soft

250g ground almonds

Egg wash from 1 egg

Grind the agar agar, sweetener and salt together in a spice grinder or coffee grinder.

Beat the eggs until smooth.

Add the powder you just made to the eggs and beat them together.

Add the coconut oil and beat well.

Add the butter and beat well again

Add the ground almonds and mix the whole lot until it is smooth and well combined.

Form the pastry into a ball and wrap in clingfilm.

Chill the pastry while you prepare to roll it out.

Line a 26cm loose bottomed tart ring using a cartouche of baking parchment or similar.

Place the tart ring on an oven proof tray.

Arrange a large sheet of clingfilm or greaseproof paper in front of you. This must be bigger than the tart will be as it will carry the pastry.

Flatten the pastry onto the clingfilm etc. with your hands and cover with another sheet of clingfilm.

Evenly roll out the pastry between the clingfilm sheets, as close as you can get to a 2mm thickness.

Peel off the top layer of clingfilm.

Pick up the pastry disc using the bottom layer of clingfilm as support and carefully invert it over the tart ring.

Gently lower the pastry onto the tart ring and with the clingfilm still on, poke it into all the corners and recesses of the mould.

Freeze the whole lot for five minutes.

Trim any excess pastry from the rim of the mold with a very sharp knife or roll over the top with a rolling pin.

Heat your oven to 140°c / gas mark 1 / 275°f.

Freeze the whole lot for another 20 minutes.

Peel off the clingfilm and prick the pastry a few times with a fork.

Bake for 35 minutes.

Remove from the oven and brush the whole inside of the pastry case with egg wash.

Return to the oven for 2 minutes.

Repeat the egg wash and baking twice more.

Remove the pastry case to cool fully in the mould.

Chocolate coconut pastry

Three people bought me a lot of coconut flour within a week of each other, so I started writing recipes to try and use the stuff up. I came up with this recipe and a few for cakes and I still have a few kilos of coconut flour in my cupboard. If only I could turn it into ice cream!

40g butter

10g coconut oil, melted

25g sweetener

1 egg yolk

1 egg

80g ground almonds

30g ground flax seed

10g cocoa powder

30g coconut flour

¼ tsp xanthan

Egg wash from 1 egg

Mix the ingredients together adding them into a bowl one by one in the order they appear in the recipe, giving the mixture a good beat with each addition.

Form the pastry into a ball and wrap in clingfilm.

Chill the pastry while you prepare to roll it out.

Line a 26cm loose bottomed tart ring using a cartouche of baking parchment or similar.

Place the tart ring on an oven proof tray.

Arrange a large sheet of clingfilm or greaseproof paper in front of you. This must be bigger than the tart will be as it will carry the pastry.

Flatten the pastry onto the clingfilm etc. with your hands and cover with another sheet of clingfilm.

Evenly roll out the pastry between the clingfilm sheets, as close as you can get to a 2mm thickness.

Peel off the top layer of clingfilm.

Pick up the pastry disc using the bottom layer of clingfilm as support and carefully invert it over the tart ring.

Gently lower the pastry onto the tart ring and with the clingfilm still on, poke it into all the corners and recesses of the mould.

Freeze the whole lot for five minutes.

Trim any excess pastry from the rim of the mould with a very sharp knife or roll over the top with a rolling pin.

Heat your oven to 140°c / gas mark 1 / 275°f.

Freeze the whole lot for another 20 minutes.

Peel off the clingfilm and prick the pastry a few times with a fork.

Bake for 30 minutes.

Remove from the oven and brush the whole inside of the pastry case with egg wash.

Return to the oven for 2 minutes.

Repeat the egg wash and baking twice more.

Remove the pastry case to cool fully in the mould.

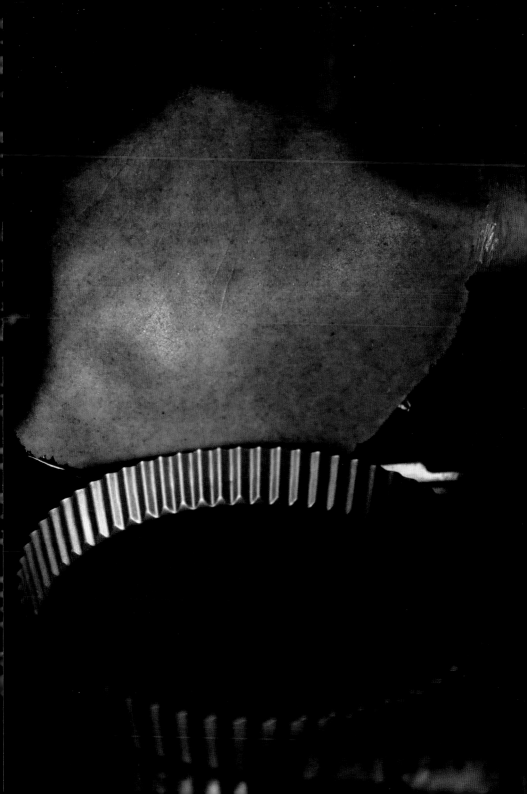

Flax seed pastry

This is one of my earlier pastry recipes, the first that really worked in any way. I had been eating a lot of my recipe development projects, and a great many were based on cream and eggs, which are not very high in fibre, so I decided to add fibre into my diet whenever I could. This happened around the time I took my first tentative steps into low carb pastry, so here we are.

100g butter, soft

50g sweetener

2 eggs

1 egg yolk

40g coconut flour

½ tsp xanthan

60g ground flaxseed

200g ground almonds

A pinch of salt

Egg wash from 1 egg

Mix the ingredients together adding them into a bowl one by one in the order they appear in the recipe, giving the mixture a good beat with each addition.

Form the pastry into a ball and wrap in clingfilm.

Chill the pastry while you prepare to roll it out.

Line a 26cm loose bottomed tart ring using a cartouche of baking parchment or similar.

Place the tart ring on an oven proof tray.

Arrange a large sheet of clingfilm or greaseproof paper in front of you. This must be bigger than the tart will be as it will carry the pastry.

Flatten the pastry onto the clingfilm etc. with your hands and cover with another sheet of clingfilm.

Evenly roll out the pastry between the clingfilm sheets, as close as you can get to a 2mm thickness.

Peel off the top layer of clingfilm.

Pick up the pastry disc using the bottom layer of clingfilm as support and carefully invert it over the tart ring.

Gently lower the pastry onto the tart ring and with the clingfilm still on, poke it into all the corners and recesses of the mould.

Freeze the whole lot for five minutes.

Trim any excess pastry from the rim of the mould with a very sharp knife or roll over the top with a rolling pin.

Heat your oven to 140°c / gas mark 1 / 275°f.

Freeze the whole thing for another 20 minutes.

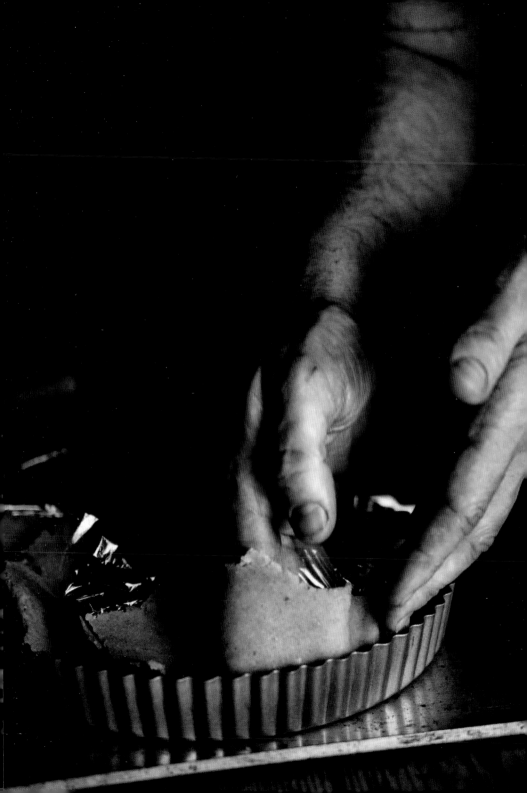

Peel off the clingfilm and prick the pastry a few times with a fork.

Bake for 35 minutes.

Remove from the oven and brush the whole inside of the pastry case with egg wash.

Return to the oven for 2 minutes.

Repeat the egg wash and baking twice more.

Remove the pastry case to cool fully in the mould.

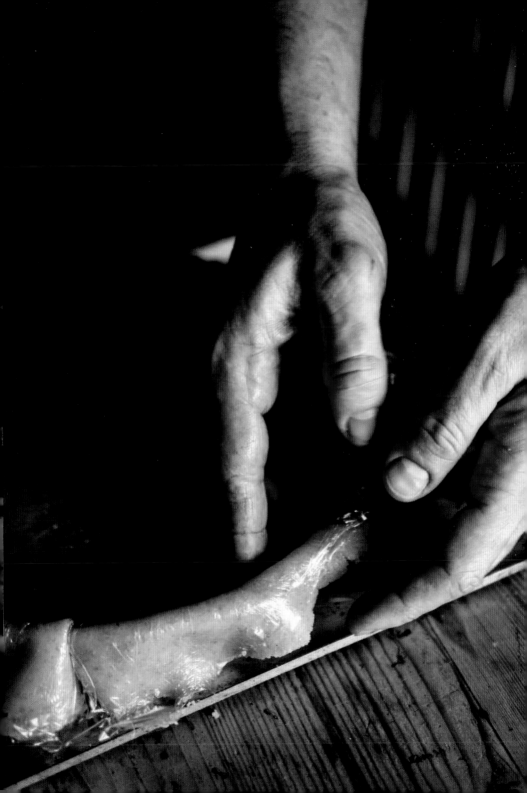

Nut butter pastry

This recipe took a long time to arrive at and was meant to be for a low carb biscuit. You can still use the recipe for biscuits if you like. It's equally good as biscuit or pastry. You could even bake it into a nice paper weight or two, it's entirely up to you, but I can only recommend it for culinary uses.

100g lard

100g tahini

150 almond butter

4 eggs

1 tsp baking powder

90g sweetener

180g ground almonds

40g coconut flour

½ tsp xanthan

Egg wash from 1 egg

Mix the ingredients together adding them into a bowl one by one in the order they appear in the recipe, giving the mixture a good beat with each addition.

Form the pastry into a ball and wrap in clingfilm.

Chill the pastry while you prepare to roll it out.

Line a 26cm loose bottomed tart ring using a cartouche of baking parchment or similar.

Place the tart ring on an oven proof tray.

Arrange a large sheet of clingfilm or greaseproof paper in front of you. This must be bigger than the tart will be as it will carry the pastry.

Flatten the pastry onto the clingfilm etc. with your hands and cover with another sheet of clingfilm.

Evenly roll out the pastry between the clingfilm sheets, as close as you can get to a 2mm thickness.

Peel off the top layer of clingfilm.

Pick up the pastry disc using the bottom layer of clingfilm as support and carefully invert it over the tart ring.

Gently lower the pastry onto the tart ring and with the clingfilm still on, poke it into all the corners and recesses of the mould.

Freeze the whole lot for five minutes.

Trim any excess pastry from the rim of the mould with a very sharp knife or roll over the top with a rolling pin.

Heat your oven to 140°c / gas mark 1 / 275°f.

Freeze the whole thing for another 20 minutes.

Peel off the clingfilm and prick the pastry a few times with a fork.

Bake for 30 minutes.

Remove from the oven and brush the whole inside of the pastry case with egg wash.

Return to the oven for 2 minutes.

Repeat the egg wash and baking twice more.

Remove the pastry case to cool fully in the mould.

Peanut butter bonbons

You may ask what stopped me from calling these little bites by the ubiquitous moniker of truffles. Being the pretentious purist that I am I decided that these little fellows were too far removed from the cream and chocolate based confections that first bore that name. Also, I like the word bonbon.

200g unsweetened almond milk

200g peanut butter, smooth

30g sweetener

30g cacao, broken up

Salted peanuts, finely crushed

Scald the first three ingredients in a small saucepan and remove from the heat.

Drop the cacao into the mixture.

Stir the cacao in until fully combined.

Pour the mixture into a tub etc. and chill in the fridge for four hours.

Portion out the bonbon balls using a warm Parisienne scoop straight into the crushed peanuts.

Roll the balls around in the peanuts until they're fully coated.

Chill the bonbons in a fridge for another hour before serving.

Blueberry compote

Compote is just the French name for fruit stewed in syrup. As with many food words it would appear to sound better in French than English, but it invariably ends up being called compost in the kitchens I have worked in. Mostly by me.

100g blueberries

40g water

15g sweetener

Add all the ingredients to a small saucepan and simmer until the water has reduced by half.

Remove from the heat to cool for ten minutes and chill in the fridge until cold.

If you are after a mushier compote, break the berries up with a fork.

Crème anglaise

The French might claim that the English don't have much imagination when it comes to food, but they are the ones who named a beautiful luscious sauce like this "English cream"!

500g single cream

45g sweetener

1 vanilla pod, seeds scraped out & removed

½ tsp vanilla extract

5 egg yolks

Put all the ingredients except the yolks in a small saucepan and slowly bring up to boiling point.

Remove from the heat to cool for five minutes.

Whisk a little of the hot cream onto the yolks to temper them and then whisk that back into the cream mixture.

Return the pan to a gentle heat and stir continuously until the sauce becomes thick enough to coat the back of a wooden spoon.

Pass the custard through a fine sieve, trying to push all the flavourful liquid out of the vanilla pod as you do.

Chill in the fridge for at least four hours with a parchment cartouche on its surface to stop a skin forming, or simply use it hot.

Mascarpone or Soured cream crème anglaise

400g mascarpone or soured cream

100g water

50g sweetener

1 vanilla pod, seeds scraped out & removed

½ tsp vanilla extract

5 egg yolks

Beat all the ingredients except the yolks together until smooth and bring to scalding point in a saucepan.

Remove from the heat and proceed in the same way as above.

Crème anglaise au beurre

"Fat bombs" have become popular for low carb diets recently, I assume that this is because people haven't heard of crème au beurre. Imagine eating a ball of coconut oil and dried coconut when you could be eating a velvety luscious concoction like this!

200g double cream

45g sweetener

1 vanilla pod, seeds scraped out & removed

½ tsp vanilla extract

4 egg yolks

200g butter, diced, cold

Scald the cream, sweetener and vanilla in a small saucepan and remove from the heat.

After five minutes, whisk a little of the cream mixture onto the yolks to temper them and then whisk this back into the pan.

Return the saucepan to a very gentle heat and whisk continuously until the custard becomes thick enough to coat the back of a wooden spoon.

Remove the saucepan from the heat.

Whisk in the cold butter cubes a few at a time.

Chill in the fridge for four hours.

Crème Chantilly

The ubiquitous original version of this recipe is widely credited to the classical French Chef Vatel. Vatel purportedly ran himself through on his own sword when he feared that the fish, he needed for a royal banquet wouldn't arrive. That's a level of commitment you don't see these days!

300g whipping cream, cold

5g sweetener

½ vanilla pod, split & seeds removed

½ tsp vanilla extract

Put all the ingredients in a bowl and whisk until it forms soft peaks.

Variations on Crème Chantilly

The possible variations are almost endless. You can add cocoa for a chocolate Chantilly, or citrus fruits, coffee, or any of the several extracts & powders etc.

Chocolate crumbs

You see a garnish which people call "chocolate soil" quite a bit; it would have to be the silliest name for a garnish I have heard, and surely not very attractive. Anyway, this is an attempt to recreate the texture without sugar etc. Or the silly name.

50g hazelnuts

25g sweetener

25g cocoa powder

25g butter, softened

A pinch of salt

Preheat your oven to 165°c / gas mark 3 / 325°f.

Blitz up your hazelnuts in a spice grinder or food processor.

Mix all the ingredients together by hand, rubbing between your fingers to create some fine parts and some slightly larger clumps.

Bake on a lined tray on the top shelf of your oven for 10 minutes, stirring halfway through.

Cool to body temperature and break up the clumps till you arrive at whatever consistancy you desire.

Store in an airtight container in the fridge or in the freezer.

You can exchange the hazelnuts for any other nut, but hazelnut and chocolate flavours work particularly well together.

Blueberry curd

If you think about it, this curd has a great deal of what you need: protein, vitamins, antioxidants, fats, micronutrients, electrolytes, some limited carbohydrates and even a little fibre. It's almost a complete and balanced meal, if you think about it. Not if you think about it in much detail though.

75g sweetener

100g butter

20g lemon juice from 1 lemon

120g blueberries

3 egg yolks

Bring the lemon juice, berries, sweetener and salt to a simmer and cook for a minute until all the fruit has softened.

Remove from the heat and add the butter.

Once melted, blitz with a hand blender and allow to cool for a minute.

Whisk in the egg yolks one by one.

Continue to whisk for a minute or so as you return the mixture to a gentle heat.

Once just thickened, remove from the heat and press through a fine sieve.

Chill in the fridge for at least four hours before use.

Variations on a Blueberry curd

Other berries like blackberries, blackcurrants and raspberries work very well in the recipe but the amount of sweetener would need to be reduced accordingly.

Strawberries work best together with a little raspberry.

Lime juice works very well here instead of the lemon.

Coconut curd

Not all coconut milks are created equal. One can buy a tin that will boil and reduce like dairy cream or one that will split at the merest hint of heat. It pays to search for the right ingredient for each job, and in this case, it pays with deliciousness.

25g coconut oil

25g sweetener

200g coconut milk (tinned)

A pinch of salt

5 egg yolks

Combine all the ingredients except the eggs in a small saucepan.

Scald the mixture and remove from the heat.

After a minute, slowly whisk a little of the liquid into the egg yolks and then whisk this egg mixture back into the saucepan.

Return the pan to a low heat and continue to whisk until the curd is thickened enough to coat the back of a spoon.

Strain through a fine sieve and chill in a fridge.

Lemon curd

Whatever genius came up with this spreadable sweetened lemon stuff deserves a big hug and I would love to give it to her/him! I imagine that in the days it was conceived the simple alchemy of a lemon becoming a velvety curd might have been associated with the supernatural, and I hope it didn't get anyone in trouble!

100g sweetener

100g butter

120g lemon juice (4 lemons)

Zest of 2 lemons, grated

5 egg yolks

Bring the lemon juice up to a simmer for a second in a small saucepan and remove from the heat.

Add the salt, zest, sweetener and butter and stir until the butter melts.

Whisk in the egg yolks one by one.

Continue to whisk for a minute or so as you return the mixture to a gentle heat.

Once just thickened, remove from the heat and press through a fine sieve.

Chill in the fridge for at least four hours before use.

Berry emulsion

I was shown the "normal" version of this by a fantastic Goan chef that I worked with. It is so perfectly clean tasting and bright that I became an instant fan. Not only that, but it is super quick too, I really don't understand how it is not more well known.

180g berries

20g sweetener, ground

180g neutral oil

Blitz the berries in a food processor.

Add the sweetener and blitz again.

Add the oil in three stages, blitzing each time.

Pass the emulsion through a fine sieve.

You can use any berries you have for this and many different oils work well in the recipe, but I usually employ a very mild pomace olive oil.

Ganache

This velvety chocolate concoction is the basis for a great many desserts and a great many moments of pleasure around the world. It took me a while to get mine right, but it was certainly worth the effort, and all the little tweaks that I made only meant that I got to eat more ganache. It's a hard life.

100g double cream

100g butter

15g sweetener

25g cacao, broken up

Place the cream, butter and sweetener in a small saucepan.

Scald the contents of the pan and remove from the heat.

Drop the broken cacao into the hot liquid and stir repeatedly until the ganache become a smooth mixture.

Transfer to a tub or mould and chill in the fridge for at least four hours.

Raspberry fluid gel

If you ever want to find something with a silly name a good bet is to look at the world of food. "Fluid gel" isn't as bad as some of the old stuff like flummery or syllabub and probably more descriptive than a lot of classical names like salmagundi or even crème anglaise. It manages however, to retain that sense of magic and mystery that calling it an agar jelly purée would somewhat lack.

350g raspberries

¼ tsp agar agar flakes

90g sweetener

150g water

¼ tsp cider or raspberry vinegar

Add all the ingredients except the vinegar to a small saucepan.

Bring to a low boil and maintain for 3 minutes.

Blitz the pan's contents with a hand blender or food processor.

Pass through a fine sieve.

Chill for two hours.

Blitz the set jelly with a hand blender or food processor.

Once set this gel will not melt again, so you can have this coulis like sauce hot if you like. Although I'm not sure why you would.

Raspberry fluid jam

I used to think that I might have preferred to have been born in some romantic past time, but in those passed times the only jams available were absolutely chocked full of sugar. These days I get to enjoy jam and my health at the same time!

160g raspberries

2 tsp agar agar flakes

2 tbsp water

2 tsp sweetener

1 tsp cider vinegar

75g raspberries

Add all the top set of ingredients to a small saucepan and mash them together with a fork.

Bring to a low boil and maintain for 3 minutes.

Blitz the pan's contents with a hand blender or food processor.

Chill for two hours.

Add the vinegar to the set jelly and blitz again.

Mash the remaining raspberries with a fork and stir them through the fluid gel

Kaya coconut jam

I came across this beautiful stuff when I was in Singapore. Traditionally it is eaten as a spread on toast, but I experienced it as a dessert garnish in several restaurants. My version is a pale imitation, but still fiendishly yummy nonetheless!

25g coconut milk powder

25g coconut oil

25g sweetener

150g coconut cream

3 egg yolks

Put the coconut milk powder and the oil in a small saucepan and gently caramelise the contents until it turns light brown and starts to clump together.

Add the coconut cream and sweetener and boil for a minute.

Transfer the contents to a food processor and blitz until smooth.

Whisk the coconut mixture onto the yolks in the same saucepan and continue to stir until thickened.

Pass through a fine sieve and chill.

Helen's nuts

I was given the basis for this recipe from a colleague who had been the pastry Chef in a Michelin starred establishment in Devon. Walnuts are not my favourite nut to eat by the handful, and I imagine they aren't yours either, but with this treatment, they really will be!

250g walnuts

25g sweetener

25g egg white (1 egg white)

2 tsp cinnamon

½ tsp mixed spice

Heat your oven to 140°c / Gas mark 1 / 275°f.

Beat the egg whites a little until they are homogenous (you are not trying to incorporate air, just make it smooth).

Mix all the ingredients together.

Spread the mixture out on a lined baking tray and bake for 1 hour, turning every 15 minutes.

Sabayon gratin

I saw this so long ago that I don't remember where, and I shamelessly poached the dish for my repertoire. Over the years I have done both sweet and savoury versions. They have been dishes with a "proper" sabayon of eggs, sugar and wine, and they have been of the simpler kind with whipped cream like this one. Honestly, considering the amount of effort involved in both recipes I think there is far more of a pay off with this one as you get to eat the food so much more quickly and your arm doesn't hurt so much!

2 tbsp kirsch or brandy

2 tbsp dry white wine

2 tbsp sweetener

A pinch of salt

3 egg yolks

100g whipping cream

Berries, rhubarb or citrus fruits

Bring the alcohol, sweetener and salt to a boil in a saucepan and reduce by half.

Remove from the heat for a minute and whisk into the egg yolks.

Whip the cream to soft peaks and fold in the egg mixture.

Arrange fruits on a heatproof plate, bowl or similar.

Spoon the creamy mix over the fruits and cook with a blowtorch or under a grill. You want a good amount of brownness on the sauce and just a little charred caramelisation on some of the fruits.

Sable thins

This is obviously not a traditional sable biscuit, but a low carb version. In French it is called sablé, meaning "sandy", because of the texture when rubbing fat and flour together. It can be used as a pastry as well as a biscuit, it is traditionally very short and not the most resilient of pastries or biscuits. In the UK we have a tradition of using the dough for thin biscuits, hence the name "thins". These are good for a variety of uses, including the biscuit base of a cheesecake, or simply to nibble on.

40g butter, soft

175g ground almonds

20g sweetener

⅛ tsp Xanthan

2 egg yolks

A pinch of salt

Beat all the ingredients together and chill, covered, for an hour.

Roll out thin and cut desired shapes.

Freeze for thirty minutes on the tray you will bake them on, lined with parchment or similar.

Heat your oven to 140°C / gas mark 1 / 275°F.

Carefully remove excess pastry from around the shapes.

Return to the freezer for ten minutes.

Bake for 25 minutes at the top of the oven.

Carefully removed from the tray onto a wire rack with a cranked palette knife, spatula or similar.

Cool for thirty minutes and store in an airtight container.

Berry sauce

I've been trying to think of a better name for this ever since I first made it. It's not a coulis. It is raw. Raw coulis? But it isn't coulis and you don't need to cook a traditional coulis, so it's back to berry sauce! Because the glycerol is only very mildly sweet and because the fruit is so gently treated there is no loss of flavour and the sauce ends up tasting fresh and vital. I'm very proud of this one, and it was all just an accident!

300g berries

100g vegetable glycerine

A pinch of salt

Place all the ingredients in a food processor and blitz.

Pass through a fine sieve to remove the seeds.

Scrape the bottom of the sieve down with a clean spoon to save as much of the fruit pulp as possible.

Variations on a berry sauce

Just raspberries makes a superb sauce, as does half strawberry and half raspberry.

Equal parts of raspberry, blackberry and blueberry is very nice

For strawberry sauce you will still need around ¼ of the berries to be raspberries

Blueberry benefits from ¼ of the berries being raspberries

Fruits of the forest mixes and black forest fruit mixes work very well in this recipe

Blackcurrants gooseberries and redcurrants work better in cooked sauces or as up to ⅓ of the berries in this recipe

Shortbread

The texture and simplicity of shortbread are very interesting to me, that such a perfect ratio would yield such perfect results makes me a little philosophical. Unfortunately, this is not shortbread, so calling it that is a little naughty but it is as nice as shortbread and "nicebread" doesn't have quite the same ring to it.

480g ground almonds

90g butter, softened

60g Truvia

30g water

1/8 tsp xanthan gum

A pinch of salt

1/8 tsp baking powder

Seeds of one vanilla pod

Replacing the vanilla with finely grated lemon zest is a nice variation. I have had lemon and rosemary too which is quite lovely.

Lavender is another traditional variation on shortbread. If you try this go easy on the lavender, or it can become soapy.

Preheat your oven to 140°c / gas mark 1 / 275°f.

Cream your butter and Truvia together.

Add the rest of your ingredients and stir until fully combined.

Roll out between two sheets of greaseproof paper. You want a thickness of about 2cm for fingers and 1cm for rounds etc.

Prick several times with a toothpick, fork or similar.

Transfer to the oven and bake on the top shelf for 30 minutes.

Cut to your desired shapes, leaving the excess where it is on the tray.

Return to the oven for another 10 minutes.

Remove from the oven and cool completely before very carefully breaking the shapes apart.

Store in an airtight container. This will freeze well.

Streusel

Something like crumble but crumblier! This German inspired recipe is traditionally a topping for Streuselkuchen, which translates as something like "sprinkle cake". I intended it to provide some texture to dishes like ice cream, chocolate mousse or anything else you like. Honestly though it's pretty good with just a spoon.

125g butter, soft

175g coconut flour

50g sweetener

A pinch of salt

Heat your oven to 140°c / gas mark 1 / 275°f.

Rub all the ingredients together and scatter on a baking tray. You want some lumps and some finer bits.

Bake for 15 minutes, gently turning every five minutes.

Leave to cool at room temperature and store in the fridge or freezer in a well-sealed container.

Brown butter Streusel

I tried to describe Streusel to a friend the other day and ended up saying "it's like crumble, but clumpier". Not really a feat of descriptive brilliance, but also not inaccurate. In German cookery there is a well-known ratio for Streusel, but that is for wheat flour and sugar, so mine is rather different.

100g butter, soft

60g sweetener

30g ground almonds

30g ground flaxseed

A pinch of salt

Heat your oven to 200°c / Gas 6 / 400°f.

Mix all the ingredients and place on a tray etc. trying to keep the mixture lumpy.

Bake for 15 minutes turning the mixture over every 5 minutes to get some even colour.

After the 15 minutes is up, remove from the oven and turn the mixture over again before leaving it to cool.

Variations on Streusel

Psyllium husks can replace half of the flaxseed if you like.

Hazelnuts are a particularly good replacement for the almonds, but any nut will do really.

Desiccated coconut makes a nice replacement for some of the flaxseed but can have a strong flavour. It pairs well with chocolate flavours and exotic fruit like passion fruit.

Crushed nuts make a nice addition, but I wouldn't add more than 30g.

Cacao nibs make a nice addition too, but again I would limit the addition to less than 30g.

Almond sponge

I was never that much of a fan of a sponge cake growing up. My mother made the best cakes for miles around and I suppose that spoiled me a little. Of course, it's totally her fault for being amazing!

30g butter, melted

1 egg

65g sweetener

150g ground almonds

1 tsp baking powder

⅛ tsp xanthan gum

3 eggs separated

Heat your oven to 165°c / gas mark 3 / 325°f.

Mix all the ingredients except the egg whites together.

Whisk the egg whites until they form soft peaks and fold them into the rest of the recipe a third at a time.

Once smoothly combined, spread the mixture onto a tray lined with greaseproof paper, to a 2cm thickness.

Bake for 20 minutes and remove from the oven to cool on a wire rack.

Chocolate truffles

You can find truffles of one form or another all over the world. Being the horribly pretentious Chef that I am though, I believe that only the most delicious, velvety smooth, indulgent confections are worthy of the name. Everything else is just balls!

100g double cream

100g butter

15g sweetener

A pinch of salt

25g cacao, broken up small

Cocoa powder or grated cacao

Bring the cream and butter up to a simmer with the sweetener and salt and remove from the heat.

Immediately add the broken-up cacao and leave to melt for a few minutes.

Stir in the warmed cacao until a glossy, harmonious chocolate ganache is formed.

Chill in the fridge for eight hours or preferably overnight.

Scoop out balls with a warm teaspoon or Parisienne scoop (melon baller), roll with your hands dusted with cocoa powder if they are not quite round enough.

Coat in the cocoa powder or grated cacao, or a mixture of both.

Variations on a truffle

Coffee truffles

Add 1½ tsp of good powdered instant coffee to the cream and butter before heating, otherwise proceed normally.

Brown butter truffles

Brown the butter in the recipe and add the cream plus another 5g to the hot butter once at the required brownness. Proceed with the rest of the recipe normally but add another 5g of cacao to the mixture.

Soured cream truffles

Swap the double cream with soured and add it to the hot butter rather than heating the two together. Then add the sweetener and salt and finally stir in the cacao as usual.

Sweetener substitutions

Truvia® My recipes are based on this as it is so readily available although often comparatively expensive.

Natvia® A stevia-erythritol blend not quite as sweet as Truvia and a little less widespread. To use this in my recipes multiply the sweetener by 1.3

Swerve® Aimed at equalling the sweetness of sugar. Simply multiply the amount of sweetener in the recipe by 2.5 and you should have a roughly correct sweetness.

Sukrin:1® Another stevia-erythritol blend but aimed at being interchangeable with table sugar so again, you would need to multiply my amounts of sweetener by around 2.5

Monk fruit. Most Monk fruit sweeteners that I see are based on erythritol and aimed at equalling the sweetness of sugar so multiply the sweetener in the recipe by 2.5 for a similar effect.

Erythritol. At around 70% the sweetness of sugar you would need to use 4.5 times the amount of sweetener in the recipe, which may have some adverse effects to the dessert and a strong laxative effect.

Xylitol. I suggest that you do not use this as it has a glycaemic index 12 times that of erythritol & stevia and it is harmful to dogs.

These are only a rough guide and some trial and error will be needed to modify the quantities I use. Everyone's palette is different, and palettes change over time becoming more or less sensitive to sweetness.

Most of the recipes should be open to an exchange of sweetener, especially if it is another stevia erythritol blend, but for the ice creams it must be the stevia-erythritol type of the same sweetness or it will affect the hardness of the ice cream.

Churchill china

https://www.churchill1795.com/

Ndali vanilla

http://ndali.net/

Meridian foods

https://www.meridianfoods.co.uk

Truvia

https://www.truvia.co.uk/

The Daisy Garland

https://www.thedaisygarland.org.uk

Diabetes UK

https://www.diabetes.org.uk

The diabetes council

https://www.thediabetescouncil.com

The Noakes foundation

https://thenoakesfoundation.org/